Dear
Mrs.
Smith

PALMETTO
PUBLISHING
Charleston, SC
www.PalmettoPublishing.com

© 2024 by Julia Novak Smith and Richard Smith

All rights reserved.
This book or any portion thereof may not be reproduced or used in any manner whatsoever without the express written permission of the publisher except for the use of brief quotations in a book review.

Hardcover ISBN: 9798822965959
Paperback ISBN: 9798822965966

Dear Mrs. Smith

A 35 year career in education for the Special Needs student

JULIA NOVAK SMITH

Contents

Least Restrictive Environment	1
Chapter 1 : Foreword	3
Chapter 2 : Foreword Shadeville Elementary School, Wakulla County, Florida	33
Chapter 3 : Foreword Sabal Palm Elementary Leon County, Florida	78
Chapter 4 : Foreword Horace O'Bryant Middle School, Key West, Florida Monroe County	104
Chapter 5 : Foreword Sigsbee Elementary Florida Keys—Florida the Accident	128
Chapter 6 : Foreword Risley Middle School, Brunswick, Georgia	142
Chapter 7 : Foreword Golden Isles Elementary School, Brunswick, Georgia	176
Foreword Washington State	218
About The Author	254

All children's and adults' names have been changed in writing this book for privacy concerns. The names of the schools, counties, and states are real.
—Julia Novak Smith

A Special Education teacher for thirty-five years
Dear Mrs. Smith
DEDICATION
AND
LEAST RESTRICTIVE ENVIRONMENT
\\\\\\\\\\\\\\\\\\\\\\\\\\\\\\\\\
\\\\\\\\\\\\\\\\\\\\\\\\\\\
Written by Julia Novak Smith A Special Education Teacher For Thirty-five Years

Dedication

The dedication of this book is especially important to me. However, I always knew if I wrote a book about my own teaching experience, to whom I would have to dedicate it. When I first met my third-grade teacher, Miss Livingston, at Bryan Elementary School, near Tampa, Florida, I was literally in awe of her!

Miss Livingston was the epitome of a loving, smart, but stern elementary teacher. When it was learning time, everyone knew it was quiet time to watch and listen. Then, when she asked questions, students always raised their hands to answer. There was no yelling out and playing around during a lesson in her classroom.

Miss Livingston had long silver braids that she wrapped around her head like a crown. She usually wore long sleeved dark dresses with the skirt ending at midcalf, usually with a white lace collar, and to complete the look, she wore black leather shoes with black laces and thick chunky heels. Even then her style of dress was considered old-fashioned and out of date.

However, to me, she looked like a queen, complete with her crown of silver hair. Miss Livingston was very proper, even regal, and I worked hard in class to please her.

She never knew how much I admired her and that I decided to become a teacher because of her when I was only eight years old!

I will never forget the impact that she made on me and my life!

Thank you, Miss Livingston!

With love,
Julia Novak Smith

Least Restrictive Environment
(How students are placed into special education programs.)

Over my years of teaching, I had so many wonderful students in my classes in each school environment in which I taught. I really enjoyed my students that I had the privilege to know and teach in all three states in which we lived for years: Florida, Georgia, and Washington.

During my career I taught students with specific learning disabilities (SLD), educable mentally handicapped (EMH), trainable mentally handicapped (TMH), emotional behavioral disordered (EBD), as well as high functioning autism (AU). Children with a specific learning disability have average or above average intelligence (IQ), which means that they should be able to learn material presented to them at least at an average rate. In some subject areas, they usually do learn at an average or above average rate. Sometimes the student may be very strong in reading/written expression skills. However, very weak, by at least two years below in math skills.

Or, it can be the opposite—at least two years below grade level in reading/written expression skills and grade level or above in math skills when measured.

Of course, standardized tests that the whole school system usually takes each year may start to show a pattern of strengths and weaknesses in each student. That is not unusual unless it is interfering with grade level learning across the board.

If this discrepancy continues to become a pattern, then usually by late second grade or early third grade, the classroom teacher would probably discuss concerns with a counselor or another person at the school with knowledge about special education.

The guidance counselor may do some initial testing, and if the pattern continues, they may call in the parents for permission for a more in-depth academic evaluation with a school psychologist.

However, the parents or legal guardians must sign the individual education plan (IEP) so that their child may be placed in a special education class or the special education teacher may come into the regular education class to provide services. The special education teacher may come into the regular education class and may work with the identified students and also some regular education students' part of the day when possible.

Chapter 1
Foreword

If a child is being considered for placement in a special education class, for even part of the school day, several requirements must be met before that can happen.

First, there would be meetings with the parents, which would probably be very concerning, and the classroom teacher or teachers, several times about the student's progress or lack thereof. Usually, the guidance counselor and others in the school that have contact with the student may want to sit in.

Then a plan would be developed and monitored to determine if the plan is helping and if progress is being made by the student. Of course, the goal is to help the student succeed in the regular education classroom if possible.

If a child is being considered for placement in a special education class, for even part of the school day, several requirements must be met before that can happen. There may be testing of the student's vision and prescribed glasses if needed.

Hearing would also be checked to make sure hearing is normal. If the hearing and vision tests are found to be in the normal range and the parents agree to testing, the academic testing may go forward. If the child is taking prescribed medication from their doctor, that would be noted.

Some preliminary testing of the student may be warranted and completed by the guidance counselor, and information would be shared about their findings.

If this has been a continuing concern, the committee, along with the parents of the student in question, must all agree to have a school psychologist test the student using the academic and psychological tests prescribed by the committee. After testing and scoring are completed by the school psychologist, all committee members would meet for the results. If an academic, emotional, or physical disability is found to be interfering with the student's ability to succeed in the usual academic setting the committee may decide the student would be better served in some type of special education program for part of the school day.

However, the placement of a child going into a special needs program can be very concerning to the parents. The committee will try to make the best informed decision for each child while considering "the least restrictive environment."

The classroom teachers and the parents may have input and concerns that they wanted addressed. The school psychologist would give their findings and discuss options for the student. If the student meets special needs program requirements, that would be discussed.

The IEP, or individual education plan, may be started at the meeting. The committee would try to make the best-informed educational decision for that individual student. If the student meets guidelines for one or more subjects for extra support in a special needs program, then the appropriate special needs teacher would be part of the committee.

The special needs teacher would be ready to explain their program and individual goals that the student would be working on in the special education classroom or even in the regular education classroom with the special education teacher going into the regular education class.

The special education teacher would explain any modifications that may be needed in regular classes as well. The regular classroom teachers and the parents may have input and concerns that they also want addressed.

The parents or legal guardians must sign the individual education plan (IEP) so that their child may be placed in a special education class, or the special education teacher may come into the regular education class to serve and work with their child in a small group part of the day when possible.

The special education teacher and regular education teacher would stay in contact with the parents through meetings and grade reports.

Carrabelle School, Carrabelle, Florida

Franklin County's history and culture are closely interwoven with the resources. In the 1,600's there were more than 40,000 Native Americans in the area. They had abundant seafood and wild animals for food, fur and skins, and freshwater rivers and streams.

The first non-natives were the Franciscan friars that arrived from Spain in the 1700's. They had come to bring the word of God and Christianity.

Apalachicola was established in 1831 and quickly grew as a cotton and fur shipping port town using steamboats. Later, Apalachicola became the county seat.

By the time of Civil War, Apalachicola was the sixth largest town in Florida with 1,906 residents.

By the late 1,800's, the railroads had expanded throughout the United States, carrying cargo farther and faster than the steamboats. As a result, the steamboats slowly disappeared and the timber industry boomed due to endless miles of forested land. Local lumber mills by the 19th and into the 20th century, in both Apalachicola and Carrabelle, produced large quantities of lumber and turpentine.

In Carrabelle, both Native Americans and early Europeans killed game for food and furs, which were shipped out. Carrabelle did well after the Civil War when lumber was a most important product to rebuild the North and the South. Probably, one of the most important people in the entire area was Dr. John Gorrie. He invented refrigeration in the form of air conditioning in the early 1850's while trying to treat malaria victims with very high fevers. Later he got a patent for his invention. There is even a small museum about the terrible malaria outbreak in Apalachicola.

Dr. Gorrie had moved from New York in 1833 to Apalachicola. He was a physician at two hospitals in the area and was active in the community. His medical research involved the study of tropical diseases, such as Malaria and some others. In 1851 Gorrie was granted a patent for a machine that made ice to help cool the fevers of his patients! Dr. Gorrie's original model of his machine is in the Smithsonian Institute.

Four years later, Dr. Gorrie died and was buried in Gorrie Square in Apalachicola, Florida, in 1855. The community named the bridge that connected Apalachicola to East Point, a small fishing village in those days, after Dr. Gorrie. Other areas in Florida have also named buildings after him as well. In fact, a school in Jacksonville, Florida, was named after Dr. Gorrie. Even a Liberty Ship built for World War II was named after Doctor John Gorrie.

In 1900, a hurricane destroyed much of the community of Carrabelle. However, the town was rebuilt and was relocated more inland where it still stands today.

***

My husband, Richard, had lived in Franklin County by himself for almost a year while I finished my Bachelor's degree at the University of South Florida, located in Tampa, Florida.

He had rented a small house in a mainly senior community called Lanark Village. It was about four miles east of Carrabelle.

The area had originally been built as a resort with a two-story hotel in the 1930s. It had a large swimming area fenced near shore where people could swim, float, or just play in the large freshwater spring that joined the salt water of the bay. Also, there was a nine-hole golf course that people enjoyed.

During World War II, Camp Gordon Johnston was built at Lanark Beach for use as an amphibious training facility, between Lanark and Dog Island. More than 25,000 trainees passed through the camp. For many, it was the last stop before going to the Pacific or European theater.

Later, after the war was over, it was turned into a senior citizen living area. Many people bought the officers' former houses and updated them, putting in new appliances, air conditioning, carpet, adding carports, sodded lawns, trees, and flowers. The nine-hole golf course, the freshwater spring, and the ocean right down the hill were also pluses.

Since rental housing was very limited, Richard lived in a small house in Lanark Village. All the elderly people loved him, and he would usually be invited to dinner or drinks in the afternoons, if he was available.

To pass the time, Richard also played baseball on two different teams and would sometimes be invited to dinner at a friend's house or go out to dinner with other Marine Patrol officers and their families.

The neighborhood in which Richard was living had a community bus that the residents could take a couple of times a week. They could sign up for a movie and a dinner trip to Tallahassee, or a trip to see a doctor and buy groceries, and so on. Of course, Richard did not use the bus; he had his Marine patrol car for work and his own personal car when he wasn't working.

I would drive up to Northwest Florida as often as I could during long weekends and breaks from college with our two-year-old son, Jason, our red and tan Doberman, Brandy, and our white poodle, Sam. My brother, Louis Wayne Novak, who was still in high school fed and watered our black cat, Amos.

Richard had been hired on April Fool's Day the year before, by the state of Florida, as a Florida Marine Patrol Officer. So, of course, Richard extolled my virtues and set up an appointment for me to meet with Mr. Haversham on my last spring break from college.

Of course, I was nervous but excited to meet with Mr. Haversham, especially when I found out that he and his wife were so well traveled. He and his wife, Marion, had worked on large cruise ships that traveled to beautiful vacation spots around the world. She announced dances, contests, races, bingo, and shows.

I was excited when Mr. Haversham offered me the elementary special education teaching position. Even the other teachers at Carrabelle School were excited! It would be the first time in over five years that there would be a certified special education teacher on the elementary side of the building!

It was a couple of months before I finished my final internship at a wonderful school in Tampa, and I would be busy finishing paperwork, etc. Then I would finally graduate from the University of South Florida in Tampa, Florida. It had been a long haul, but now I could "see the light at the end of the tunnel!" and would graduate one quarter earlier due to the heavy load I carried trying to get back to Richard in North Florida in the spring.

Sometimes, Richard would catch a free ride from Carrabelle on a Greyhound bus to Tampa, where I would pick him up at the Greyhound bus station. The bus drivers always liked to have him on board, knowing he was a state officer with a gun, just in case there was a robbery! It was exciting to see him getting off the bus after a long time apart. Plus, Jason and Brandy, our Doberman Pincer, were always thrilled to see Daddy!

After I picked Richard up, we would catch up on mail, bills, and just being together, which was wonderful! We had a contract for our two-year-old home in Tampa, and the new owners would be moving in soon. So, I moved back into my old bedroom, in my parents' house, one mile away, but, with a new addition, our two-and-a-half-year-old little boy, Jason.

I drove up to North Florida once again, but this time for the closing on our new house on Alligator Point (named for the shape of the small peninsula of land on the water in Franklin County). Once again with Jason, Brandy, and this time our black cat, Amos, who was not happy in a crate!

After a few days at our new home, Jason and I had to go back and stay with my parents in their home for another week to finish my internship. When we were leaving, Amos, our black cat, climbed to the top of a tall tree and wouldn't come down. In fact, Amos wouldn't come down for a whole week! When Jason and I came back, Amos immediately climbed smartly down the tree and meowed and rubbed against my legs! I had given my new address to USF so that the university could mail my diploma to my Alligator Point address, so after all that, I didn't get to walk but, had been hired in the spring, and that was great!

We bought a small center console boat and motor and loved going to Dog Island with Jason and our dog, Brandy. The only way to get there was by boat, or small plane, so most people never went to the beautiful, isolated island.

There were a few beach houses on stilts and one screen house on stilts. So, usually during the week we would be by ourselves on Dog Island. We could let our Brandy run around, sniff, dig, and just have a great time!

We looked for shells, hermit crabs, sea urchins, and interesting pieces of wood that had been tumbled by sand and sea until smooth.

Sometimes we would fish and then have a picnic lunch on the beach. Good times were had by all!

We also would occasionally go to St. George Island by boat. There was also a bridge to the island from Apalachicola. Several teachers from Carrabelle School lived on St. George Island and rode to school together. We would usually see people looking for shells, fishing from the dock, and just having a good time. However, we had to keep Brandy on a leash when she was with us. On this island there were cars and trucks and ferries coming and going!

The first day of teachers' workdays, before the students started the 1977–78 school year, all the teachers were talking about Elvis Presley dying! Most of us had heard the news on the way to the school on our car radios. We were all shocked! At least we all had something in common to discuss and bond with each other about.

As I looked around my beautiful and bright first classroom as a brand-new teacher, I marveled that I had finally reached my goal of many years from the time I was eight years old! I had finally become a certified teacher in exceptional education, or special education, as it is now usually called.

I thought back to a few months earlier when I had been interviewed and hired on my last spring break from college by Mr. Haversham, my first principal, as an elementary special education teacher! I was ecstatic!

In the past few years, there had been a home economics teacher in the elementary special education position. She cooked her dinner in the classroom every day and washed and dried her clothes during class as well! She was able to do that because there was a complete kitchen and laundry area set up in the special needs classroom! She slept in her car most nights in the school parking lot!

When Mr. Haversham found out, all the appliances were immediately moved out! Then, a librarian took the position.

When I found out, I was worried that everyone would expect miracles from me right away because, I was "certified. "I was worried and felt unprepared and thought that I might let them and myself down!

I had never thought that I would have such a large, beautiful classroom, complete with two bathrooms! My room was well stocked with all kinds of equipment that was state of the art at that time in August 1977. I even had a great color TV on a cart and a new VCR! Most homes didn't have them in the late seventies, and certainly most families in Carrabelle didn't. However, you could rent VCR's and tapes from large grocery store chains in Tallahassee.

I knew that Franklin County was the poorest county in the state of Florida, and Carrabelle School had been built by the federal government because of that. That wasn't all! The school was air conditioned, filled with all new furniture, many supplies and materials, great lighting, carpeted floors, and most of the hallways were closed in.

Even though I had finally achieved my goal of becoming a special needs or special education teacher, or even known as an exceptional education teacher, sometimes I would still get homesick for the Central Florida area and especially Tampa, Florida. Most of my family lived and worked there as well as Richard's family and friends.

Even in the late 1970's, the Tampa-Saint Petersburg-Clearwater area was a large metro statistical area. The area had over three million residents, a busy port and shipyards, with beautiful white sand beaches, many beautiful hotels and motels, wonderful restaurants, great public and private universities, community colleges with many different campus sites, and business schools.

A large attraction, Busch Gardens, was established in Tampa. At that time, it was free, but you had to pay one dollar ($1.00) to park your vehicle. There was also a new football stadium, with a professional football team and many professional baseball teams that came to the Tampa Bay area and the surrounding areas for spring training.

There were lots of parks, zoos, golf courses, lots of shopping venues, and even the first enclosed shopping mall in the state, West Shore Plaza, which was where I loved to shop!

MacDill Air Force Base was in Tampa, as well as the Tampa Municipal Airport.

At the time, Tampa was ranked the fifth most popular American city for travel, work, and play. So, I was used to larger cities, not a tiny community without even one red light in Carrabelle, Florida, and only one in the Franklin County seat in Apalachicola, Florida.

There were no name brand department stores or even a name brand fast-food restaurant anywhere in the area! You could go to the local pharmacy in an old building in the little town of Carrabelle with a screen door and just an old fan that barely circulated the warm air, even in the hot summer. Or you could go to the small, old fashioned family grocery store with a screen door and no air conditioning, take your pick! The grocery store was in a time warp-dark and dusty. However, you could still buy a piece of candy for two cents! Or, if you were hungry, you could buy a reddish-purple pickled egg floating in a big vinegar jar for fifteen cents! Or you could buy a big red sausage floating in a jar of some red fluid for a quarter! The students would be excited and wanted to show me before class what they were having for breakfast: the purple egg or the big red sausage! They were generous and would always tell me how good it was and would want to share it with me! I always would thank the kids that offered me some of their food. However, I would thank them for offering but told them that I had eaten a big breakfast, which was not exactly true, unless a piece of toast with half of a banana is a huge breakfast!

However, there were some seafood restaurants that served fresh and delicious fried shrimp, fish, oysters, crabs, or scallops with the usual sides: slaw or salad, French fries or grits, or maybe baked potatoes and hushpuppies. I never knew why they called fried cornmeal about the size of a spoon without the handle until much later in my life. It was because in the south, where it is so hot, the kitchen was separated from the main house to try to keep the rest of the house cooler. So, the hunting dogs would go out to the cooks' kitchens and would whine and bark so the cooks would throw them some fried cornmeal to make them hush! So, the hushpuppy was born!

After dinner, and if you were lucky, and Julie Mae's Restaurant still had some freshly made pies, you would be in luck! The coconut cream pies were fabulous, as were the chocolate cream, and usually didn't last long in the refrigerator case! Plus, there were usually apple crumb and a few more in the pie safe. The pies were sold by the generous slice.

One day around lunchtime, a boy from a fourth-grade classroom told me that his teacher wanted me to go the lunchroom and get a student that we both shared, Johnny Valley, off the lunchroom table!

Well, to be friendly, I decided to go to the lunchroom and check on Johnny. Yes, he certainly was on the middle of the round table...dancing!!

The kids who were trying to eat were upset and were yelling at him as he laughed and kept dancing!

I walked over to him and told him to get down, or I would have to embarrass him as I grabbed him off the table. Johnny didn't get off, so "I helped him safely off the table," and took him to my room. I told the student who had come to my room earlier to come and get him when lunch was over. Then, I didn't worry anymore about the incident, until the next morning.

The next morning, Johnny came to my classroom, with a letter in his hand and a smile on his face.

I thought his mother must have found out about Johnny dancing on the lunch table. Now she had written a nice thank you note to me for making sure he was safe.

When I finally opened the envelope, I was savoring my first written communication with one of my first year' student's parents. I was expecting a nice thank you or something along those lines. As I unfolded the letter, I read the date at the top right corner and then looked down and read, "Dear Mrs. Smith, "the salutation was in beautiful cursive writing. It was also placed in the correct area on the page. Great so far! I had been warned about uneducated parents who could barely write their name much less, set up a friendly letter correctly.

I am sure my smile disappeared, and my eyes opened wide as I read something like this:

> "Dear Mrs. Smith,
> You better not touch my boy again! I am the best bar fighter in town (Carrabelle, FL). You can ask anybody! If you do touch him, I will beat you up and pull out as much of that blond hair as I can!"

Then she signed the letter correctly with a friendly closing:
"Love, Lindy"

When I recovered, my face was probably red with embarrassment and shock because I had been bodily threatened!! As I looked at fourth grade Johnny, who continued to smile, I was flabbergasted! All I had done was try to get her son out of harm's way while he was dancing on the table!

I had never met anyone who bragged about being "the best bar fighter in town" and had never been threatened like that in my life!

Well, finally, I did manage to thank Johnny for giving me the "nice" letter from his "sweet mother" and asked him to thank his mom for me as I smiled. However, all I could think about was Johnny's mother and her promise!

At lunchtime, I went to see my principal and showed him the letter, even though I was embarrassed. He chuckled, as he read the letter! However, I didn't think it was funny! I told him if someone found me knocked out cold on my classroom floor one day, remember Mrs. Valley and her bar fighting experience!

We both laughed. However, I was more than a little nervous. Oh, the reason Johnny's mom had threatened me. It was because I removed Johnny from the round lunch table in the lunchroom. Go figure!

As I walked out of Mr. Haversham's office, he said, "You know, I have heard that Johnny's mother is the best bar fighter in town!" as he laughed!

I left the letter with my principal. Now, I'm sorry I did. I could have framed it! I was impressed with her beautiful cursive writing ability! I found out that a lot of parents couldn't write, or even sign their own name! When I conducted meetings, which were required when an individual education plan (IEP) was developed or updated, which must be done at least yearly, a number parents could not even write their name. The first year as a teacher in Carrabelle, I was usually pleasantly surprised if they could read, and about half of my parents could at least sign their name by themselves. When I had a meetings with a student's parents, both parents would usually come and be on time. Even the parents who could not read or write would usually be there and on time. When the parents came to a meeting with me, I tried to have a positive attitude and not embarrass them if they couldn't write their names.

One morning, Carrabelle, Florida, was on the nationally syndicated "The Today Show." Later, it was featured on several other television shows such as "Real People" and "Ripley's Believe It or Not." The Carrabelle Police Department finally made the big time, in all its glory as "The World's Smallest Police Station!" Plus, the smallest police station has been seen in several movies!

The shows filmed the police department in Carrabelle! I really couldn't believe it when Richard showed me the official police department! It was a regular old-fashioned telephone booth, complete with the folding doors on the side of the road. The difference was that it had "POLICE" written at the top of the doors. and it had been painted "police blue." Most of the time, a police officer would be sitting in his car waiting for a phone call, while he did his reports, etc.

Yes, it was just like the booths that used to be on many streets across America in those days! The way it worked was that when someone needed police assistance, they could call the phone number on the phone booth. However, the call was free. A policeman would then try to take care of the citizen's problem. At that time there were three police officers in Carrabelle, each working eight-hour shifts, plus a police captain.

My husband, Richard, introduced me to a friend of his, John. He was one of the police officers in Carrabelle. At the time I met John, he knew I was about to finish my teaching degree and would be moving to the area in about six months. So, since he and his family had just moved out of a rental house and bought a new home, he still had his rental house keys. So, he showed the house to us inside and out. Shortly after meeting him, Richard and I decided we would rather buy a place so we wouldn't have to move again.

One night Richard called me in Tampa and told me about a tragedy that had upset him. The police officer that had shown us the rental house a couple weeks before responded to a call involving domestic abuse. The grandfather who owned the house and was on the front porch with his severely handicapped grandson was threatening to kill his grandson while other family members watched. After arriving, Police Officer David Patton was ultimately killed by the grandfather while exiting his patrol vehicle. After killing Police Officer Patton, the grandfather ran to the back yard and took is own life. It was a horrible end to a nice young man with two children, and his wife.

Occasionally we would go down to visit our families in the Tampa area, or our families would come to visit us, but I had a full-time position teaching now! I had lesson plans—Individual Education Plans for each student—that I had to write and keep updated. I was usually tired after a long week of teaching eighteen to twenty-five students on my caseload, and talking with parents and classroom teachers, and trying to be helpful to everyone.

During the first year of teaching, we tried to go to Tallahassee usually every Friday afternoon when I got home from school. We usually ate out, sometimes at the famous Brown Derby in Tallahassee, then shop a little, and last, buy groceries at a nice grocery store, usually the Tallahassee Publix Super Market at the North Wood Mall. We would always carry a cooler for refrigerator and freezer foods. Then, we would go home, to relax, and play with Jason and Brandy. Usually we would plan on going out on our boat on Saturday!

We liked where we lived. We were just a short walk to the saltwater bay where we kept our three crab traps. There were a couple of other houses where the owners lived year-round. There were a few houses that were summer and weekend places for mainly teachers and professors. We mainly socialized with a few state officers and their young families on the weekends.

Most of the students in my special education classes were wonderful and just poor, but sweet kids. Most of their parents were happy to have a certified young teacher with lots of new ideas of how to keep the kids on target and working towards their individual educational goals. The parents wanted their children to learn to read and write even though many of the parents couldn't even write their names.

Years later in my career, I found that most parents admired teachers and thanked me for helping their children. Like most parents, they wanted a better life for their children than they had.

I usually had between eighteen and twenty-five students that I taught on a daily schedule. These children with special needs were from kindergarten through fifth grade. Some came to my room for an hour or maybe two hours per day. Others might stay longer if they had more severe educational or emotional needs. Then they would go back to their regular grade level classes.

I admit I was surprised when I first met my students. I read their psychological testing reports to find out what kind of learning issues they presented.

Remember, there was no other special needs teacher on the elementary side of the school-just me! Plus, another brand new male special needs teacher on the middle through high school side as well. I really learned a lot during my first two years of teaching. I have to say it was quite an experience! I had a second- grade student named Tommy, with Tourette's syndrome, and Tommy was always licking the walls or putting unusual things in his mouth. Plus, sometimes he would try to swallow weird things that he sneaked into his mouth!

One day, I caught Tommy with a short piece of dark blue yarn hanging about two inches out of his closed mouth. I made him open his mouth, and I used a Kleenex to pull it out. However, I pulled and pulled on the yarn, and it kept sliding out covered in thick saliva. I finally was able to pull out almost three feet of slimy yarn! I always had a weak stomach about things like that, but thank goodness I didn't throw up, even though I thought I might be sick after that experience!

I met many wonderful parents, teachers, and students and had great fun learning with the students! During my second year of teaching, I received a truly brilliant five-year-old kindergarten student. She was not only very bright, but very precocious! She didn't have any hair on her head including her face! Why? She pulled it out including eyelashes and eyebrows! When I tried to talk with her about why she did it, Laura was very frank with me and said, "Because it frustrates my mother!" Then I asked her why she wanted to frustrate her mom, and she told me, "Because she divorced my dad!" I had her in my class to try and connect emotionally with her. She was functioning several years above grade level, and I tried to interest Laura in activities and hobbies that she could concentrate on and just be a little girl for a while. She seemed to be happier and reminded her kindergarten teacher when it was time to go to my classroom. She wore a watch and could tell time in kindergarten!! I felt we both made some real progress, and she started smiling when she came into my room and loved to talk to me. I didn't judge her; I didn't even mention her hairless face and scalp. She was suffering from the loss of her father from the family unit due to the divorce. Even though she was mentally gifted, she was still just a five-year-old child grieving for her daddy lost from the family unit and didn't know why her parents divorced.

Her mom was very worried about her daughter, and rightly so; however, she projected her worry on her only child because they were now a two-member family, and she blamed her ex-husband for their daughter's problems!

I loved my students, and I wanted to help them have a better life. I had a brother and sister both in the same grade because Benny had been held back twice before he was tested and placed in a special needs class for mental disabilities or mentally handicapped. However, Sara, and her younger brother, was diagnosed with a specific learning disability. Even though Benny was two and a half years older, he was about a foot shorter. Sara and Benny were sweet children and loved school.

However, they were very poor black children, and Sara was about my size. So, I asked her to ask her mom if I could give her some of my clothes I didn't need anymore. Of course, her mom said, "Yes, and thank you! So, I gave Sara a very nice gray wool coat with a big fur collar, plus some of my blouses and pants.

Sara was so proud and wanted to make sure I noticed what she was wearing. I can remember her on the playground before school—Sara and Benny walked to school and usually got there early. In the early mornings during the winter, it was freezing, and many times there would be heavy frost all over the ground.

Poor Benny was just a sweet little guy. After school he would hurry home to get his BB gun and kill as many doves as he could. He had a little business; several of the older black ladies in their neighborhood would buy all the doves he got for a dime a piece. The ladies would clean and cook them for dinner. I must admit I was shocked, but I didn't say anything against his business.

We did love the area most of the time! It was new and certainly different from how we had grown up. However, we both had always loved salt water. Usually, we would go fishing in my parents' boat in the Tampa, St. Petersburg, and Tarpon Springs areas.

Many times, while I was growing up, and even afterwards when I was grown, my Hungarian grandfather Charles Novak would go fishing with us in my mom and dad's boat. Granddad was always fun and had a great time on the boat! He always laughed as he reeled in the fish!

Now we lived almost on salt water. We just had to walk a short path to the bay where we kept our crab traps.

It was interesting! We even found broken shards of old Native American pottery and some ancient arrow heads. It was fun for our beautiful Doberman Pincer, too! However, when we checked our crab traps, we had to be careful about our Doberman, Brandy. She was interested in the creatures that we dumped into a big bucket—one time, too interested! She stuck her head in the bucket and went down on her knees, making a terrible keening sound! A blue crab had locked on her sensitive nose!

Finally, we realized what was happening, and my husband, Richard, was able to knock the crab off her nose with a thick glove! Poor Brandy, however, she soon got over the pain and became her fun-loving self again!

Brandy did learn a great lesson though and never stuck her head in the crab bucket again!

Richard, Jason, Brandy, and I had so much fun on our center console boat exploring the waterways and several small islands in the area. Dog Island and St. George Island were favorite places for us.

Sometimes we would just pull our crab traps or find a live oyster bed in the bay and break off some live salty oysters. Also, we would fish or just ride around in our small boat and have a picnic on a small beach.

There really wasn't much else to do there. However, we had fun times on the saltwater. Sometimes we would even have company with us—like a large alligator tagging along with us on our boat! Then we would usually leave. Yes, alligators will swim in salt water!

One morning, I had the children working quietly in the classroom while I was conducting a small reading group. As I looked around, I was so impressed with the students as they independently and quietly worked at their seats.

Then, a ten-year-old boy yelled, "Hey, someone's cutting the cheese!" Then, I asked, "Why is anyone eating cheese in my room, and why do they have a knife? Give me the cheese and the knife right now!" However, everyone laughed! Then one of the boys said, "No, Mrs. Smith, they're farting!" I had to admit that I had never heard that before! That afternoon when I went home, I told Richard about the "cheesy incident," and he just laughed! He couldn't believe that I had never heard that phrase!

Another day in my classroom, there was more excitement! David, who was in fifth grade came into my room with a thin leather shoelace tied around his neck and was showing off something dangling from it like a pendant. It was a kind of small bone from some unfortunate animal. The boys were uproariously laughing about it. I should never have asked what kind of bone it was, because he told me! It was actually a bone from a racoon's penis! The boys all thought it was so hilarious! However, I had never heard of such a thing and just tried to ignore it. I told him if the necklace was going to interfere with his classwork and my math lesson, then his father would be called to come and get the necklace after school. After all, his father was a trapper and hunter. Later when Jason and I got home, I asked Richard if he knew David's dad; he told me that he had met him and knew some animals had penis bones.

During my second year of teaching, my brother Louis Wayne Novak came from Tampa to live with us. He attended Carrabelle High School.

Every school day I had to get him up; sometimes I almost had to drag him out of bed! He had always been a heavy sleeper.

Louis had his own bedroom and bathroom downstairs, and we had three bedrooms and a bathroom upstairs.

After I got Louis up, I had to run back upstairs and get Jason dressed for nursery school. I had to get both boys up very early because I had to drive through a national forest on lonely roads to take our son, Jason, who was now three and a half years old, east to a great nursery school in the next county and then retrace my miles back to Carrabelle School every school morning. My brother would barely have his clothes on and would eat and drink a glass of milk in my car and would usually sleep through most of the trip. Sometimes my husband, Richard, could pick Jason up; however, usually I would have to retrace my miles from the morning drive and pick Jason up in the afternoons as well.

Louis built a small wooden boat in shop class, and when it was finished, my brother Louis, Jason, and I would get in the sturdy black boat and paddle a short distance to our crab traps in our little cove. Brandy would stay on shore and bark at the crabs as they were dumped in a bucket! It was always fun! However, Brandy had learned her lesson about crabs' pinchers!

Afterword
Carrabelle School, Franklin County, Florida

When I moved to Franklin County, Florida, to begin my teaching career after graduating from the University of South Florida, I thought I was ready!

I worked on my wardrobe all summer. I bought some nice high heels in pretty colors with purses to match. My mother-in-law, who loved to sew, made some beautiful outfits for me. I also made some clothes and bought some in Tallahassee.

I was ready and excited! When I was in Tampa and some surrounding cities, I was expected to always dress professionally at the schools where I interned.

However, I found out most of the teachers in northwest Florida seemed to believe in a more relaxed and comfortable look (jeans and T-shirts) for male and female teachers.

In fact, a male teacher told me that it wouldn't be too long until I started to dress down and give up the high heels and makeup, etc. He told me the same thing had happened to his mother when she had moved from a big city to poor Carrabelle!

Years later, I saw him at Florida State University in Tallahassee where I was finishing my master's degree. I was still dressed nice, complete with high heels and makeup!

Years later, I found out that Johnny Valley climbed onto a counter in one of his middle school classes with a pair of scissors in his hand. As he jumped off the counter, the scissors stabbed through another student's palm of his hand as he tried to shield his eyes and face! Johnny was suspended for a week that time.

Later, in high school, Johnny shot the principal of the school with a pellet rifle in his back! That time he was finally expelled from public school!

After that, I lost track of him. With Johnny Valley, it was hard to be surprised about anything he might do! I just hope that he grew up and emotionally matured enough to be a contributing citizen wherever he lives now.

If you have forgotten who Johnny Valley was, he was the student whose fourth-grade teacher sent a note to me at lunchtime, to please get him down from the lunch table as he danced in the middle of it. Then, the next morning I received a "lovely letter" threatening me that if I ever touched him again, she would pull all my blond hair out! Plus, she bragged she was the "Best Bar Fighter in Town!"

There were many other interesting incidents in those two years. It would take another whole book to list them all. Let's just say I got a real education in my first two years of teaching!

In my second year of teaching, my principal, Mr. Haversham, who was a great guy and who had hired me, and two full-time paraprofessionals for my class, had a stroke in his office during the school day.

At the time it happened, Mr. Haversham was discussing some issues with long time teachers at Carrabelle School. While he was talking over the problems with a few of their students and something else going on that needed to be addressed, he became unresponsive!

Mr. Haversham was taken by ambulance to the hospital in Tallahassee about two hours away.

Several weeks later, our principal was able to return home but became very despondent and ended his life later that year. He was well loved and was a good man.

My husband and I recently finished our latest motor home trip to northwest Florida in February 2023. It had been many years since we had visited the area! Many places are now unrecognizable! There are few seafood houses that still sell fresh caught fish, shrimp, or scallops. I didn't see any local oyster houses. There are still a few bars, and the police phone booth is still there!

My first school, where I started my exceptional education or special education career, has been closed for many years! There is no school in Carrabelle anymore. There is only one modern and beautiful school in Franklin County now, which goes from kindergarten through high school. This way, they can have a larger pool of athletes and scholars. So, now Carrabelle and Apalachicola team up to play other schools in the closest counties! I was really surprised; however, it makes sense!

Chapter 2
Foreword

Shadeville Elementary School, Wakulla County, Florida

Wakulla County's seat, Crawfordville, is the only unincorporated county seat among Florida's 67 counties.

In 1528, Spanish explorer Panfilo de Narvaez determined that where the Wakulla and Saint Marks Rivers met, would be a superior location for a military fort. A few years later, Hernando de Soto's expedition passed through Florida on a similar route. The wooden fort was named Fort San Marcos de Apalachee in the late 1600s. A stone fort was started but was not finished in the 1760s when Great Britain took over. Twenty years later, the Spanish returned. A former British officer named William Augustus Bowles tried to unify and lead 400 Creek Indians to push the Spanish out of San Marcos and temporarily captured the fort. Five weeks later,

Spanish ships arrived and took back control of the fort and area.

In 1818, General Andrew Jackson recaptured Fort San Marcos and two British citizens. They were tried and found guilty of inciting Indian raids. They later were executed.

This caused a diplomatic feud between the United States and Great Britain. The United States garrison of 200 infantry and artillery men gained control of the fort for close to a year in 1818-1819.

By 1839, the Federal Government took over and built a merchant marine hospital. The hospital provided care for seamen and local yellow fever victims.

Wakulla County was created from a part of Leon County, where the capitol of Florida was in the city of Tallahassee.

During the Civil War, Wakulla County was blockaded from 1861 to 1865 by a Union Navy squadron at the mouth of the Saint Marks River. The Battle of Natural Bridge (which is a place where the Saint Marks River goes underground) eventually stopped the Union troops that had intended to take over the fort, whose name had been changed to Fort Ward (Saint Marks).

The Confederate Army had fewer soldiers, however, they had over a day to ready their defenses, and the Union Army retreated. Many of Wakulla County's residents lived in poverty in the early 1800s.

During this time, many people in Wakulla County hunted animals for their furs and "tapped" pine trees to get their valuable pine tar or pine sap to sell. When these products were sold, they were loaded on riverboats and then onto larger ships.

Later, when train tracks were constructed over land and rivers, trains could travel through the thick forests more efficiently than many of the river boats, and they became obsolete. Also, pine sap and furs were transported by train to larger cities for refinement and then for sale.

Wakulla County's greatest natural attraction is Wakulla Springs, which is one of the world's largest freshwater springs, both in terms of depth and water flow. In 1974, the water flow was measured at 1.23 billion US gallons per day! The greatest recorded flow ever for a single spring! The spring is nearly round and measures some four hundred feet in diameter, and its depth is about one hundred and fifty feet. The water is extremely clear. So clear, that underwater scenes of several movies and commercials have been filmed in and around the spring over the years.

***

At the end of the second school year at Carrabelle School (K–12), I was excited because I now felt much more comfortable as a teacher. I had completed two school years in my own special needs classroom and had taught three different exceptionalities throughout the day—sometimes at the same time in my classroom. I had learned a lot about teaching and life from many of my students and their parents.

However, we were transferred to Wakulla County by request. We had decided that we needed to be closer to Tallahassee, which meant hospitals, doctors, more shopping options, and Florida State University, all of which were only about an hour to an hour and a half away.

Remember, we were pregnant with twins, which would mean a lot of pediatrician appointments and daycare after they arrived!

We were having a new home built in a nice family neighborhood in Wakulla County, and it would still take several more months before it would be completed. After we sold our two-story beach house at Alligator Pointe, we rented a small beach house on stilts whose owners lived in Tallahassee most of the time. They assured us that they didn't plan to use the beach house for a long while. However, they later decided that they would like to come down and stay for several months. So, we had to move again! This time, we moved to Crawfordville, in Wakulla County, closer to Tallahassee and much closer to our new home that was under construction.

The rental house was a small little cottage with a nice lawn and a few trees, where our five-year-old son, Jason, could play outside. Since it was only temporary, we kept most of our household items packed in big boxes. So, we had to navigate the hallways and rooms carefully because there were boxes and new furniture stacked everywhere!

Before I gave birth, the special education administrator of Wakulla County, Mr. Jackson, had talked to someone about me from Carrabelle School in Franklin County. Mr. Jackson found out where we had moved temporarily into the county and knew the "Tully House"! It seemed everyone else did, as well!

After a few minutes, Mr. Jackson offered me a great teaching position beginning in the fall semester at a higher salary, and I immediately took the offer! I was embarrassed because my skin and even my hair were damp and oily with perspiration from the heat and humidity! I was dressed in a huge maternity sundress and standing with bare feet on the front porch of the Tully rental house!

Mr. Jackson still hired me! Dr. Melpomene Swafford, my lead professor at the University of South Florida in Tampa, always advised, "Always dress well and neat, well-groomed, and act confident."

After I had been hired, even though I broke every one of Dr. Swafford's rules, I was excited! I didn't have to worry about a teaching position anymore! I knew where I would be teaching, Shadeville Elementary School! Also, I would be making more money than I had ever earned in my life!

A few days later, I heard another knock at the front door and again, someone was walking on the front porch. This time, when I went to the screen door, I met a sweet lady named Yvonne. Again, my clothes and hair were damp with perspiration, and I was walking around with bare feet, because I could barely fit into my sandals or flip flops anymore because my feet were so swollen from pregnancy and the heat!

Ms. Yvonne had decided to drop by because she was starting a new daycare business in her just completed new home and had heard that my family and I had just moved into Wakulla County. In small towns, people usually talked about other new people, especially since we were originally from Tampa and I was pregnant with twins. I had just been hired as a special needs teacher at Shadeville Elementary for the coming school year, so people had something new to talk about. Ms. Yvonne already had one little two-year-old girl who would be in her care during the coming school year. My two babies would make three children! Perfect!

Another problem was that I couldn't see my feet anymore when I walked through the rental house or on the lawn with Jason. Sometimes I would almost fall inside the little cottage. So, I would sort of bump into things like bumper cars at the county fair!

There was another big problem, there was NO AIR CONDITIONING! and we were living in the hottest part of the summer in the little cottage! So, I did have a couple of fans that helped some especially if I sprayed myself with a water bottle.

One more problem, I had to stop taking baths-only showers because the last time I sat in the tub, I literally could not get out!! My husband could not get a grip on me because, "I was slippery when wet!" Richard had finally put some dry beach towels around me, and as five-year-old Jason started getting upset, thinking I was hurt, Richard hoisted me up and out! Then Jason, with a mop of blond hair, jumped up and down while clapping his hands!

Another problem had been that the house was old, however in good repair. When the house had originally been built maybe close, to one hundred years ago, a bathroom was not seen as a place to luxuriate in a tub for an hour or so in a small farming, hunting, and fishing community. It was a place to clean up and get out quick for the next family member to have a turn! The bathroom was small and the sink was across from the toilet, there was barely enough room for one average sized person, much less two people one of whom was hugely pregnant with twins! Lots of times we would go out for dinner, but it was a small place with few choices. So, sometimes we would eat outside at the picnic table on the back lawn under some nice shade trees, especially where it would be cooler than inside—if I had cooked!

Finally, one week before I gave birth, we moved into our new home! Our builder, John Shuff, had promised that we would be in our new home before the twins arrived, and we were, but just barely!

Even though we were now in the new house, the finish carpenters were still working on the trim work, light fixtures, touch up painting, putting on inside doors, hardware, building a patio roof, etc. The carpenters were worried that I might go into labor and begged me to please stay seated when they were there, since I was overdue with twins and huge!

I could not even sit up normally! Also, it was hard to breathe since I had one baby down low and one up high pressing on my left lung. At my next visit to my wonderful doctor, my gynecologist-obstetrician, Dr. Stewart told me that I had to go to the hospital in Tallahassee for a Caesarian Section! He told me that he didn't think I would ever go into labor naturally. Of course, we were excited, but nervous, so we called both of our families!

Then, the next day, August 23, I was admitted to the hospital in Tallahassee and gave birth on August 24th. Adrien was born first at 12:29 and weighed six pounds and four ounces and measured twenty inches. Then Arien was born one minute later at 12:30 and weighed seven pounds and two ounces and was twenty inches long, as well. However, Adrien's umbilical cord was drying up, and she was losing weight. So, Dr. Stewart made a good choice to go ahead with the C-section!

While I was in the hospital, before our babies were born, Richard's parents drove up from Lakeland, Florida. When Richard's dad drove back home, Richard's mother stayed with Jason and helped him get ready for first grade every day. She usually cooked dinner most nights in our new kitchen. Then one time, while I was still in the hospital, Richard brought a piece of chocolate cake that his mom had baked. It was greatly appreciated, since hospital food usually wasn't very appetizing!

My mother, dad, and my dad's Hungarian parents drove from Tampa, Florida, to Tallahassee, to visit for a couple of hours with our twin girls and me at the hospital.

Finally, after visiting with the twins (Miss A and Miss B at the time, because we couldn't settle on two girls' names), they all came into my room to see me and brought a beautiful bouquet of red roses in a silver vase. My parents brought two puffy light blue dresses with a white ruffle around the bottom. Also, they gave the girls each a plush toy animal that had a music box inside their bodies. My grandparents gave us two nice cards with money in the envelopes. It was a short but sweet visit.

My family returned to Tampa the same day. My father had to travel to Kansas City on business the next day. We were almost overwhelmed with two newborn baby girls! I had just had major surgery! My doctor kept me in the hospital for an entire week, and even then, he told me he hated sending me home because it would be "like a war zone for a while!" After a week, the girls and I got out of the hospital. My sweet mother-in-law decided to stay one more week. She bought each of the girls a beautiful pale-yellow puffy dress and white lacy socks. Arien and Adrien didn't seem to like to dress up! As we were leaving the hospital, the sweet nurses were smiling and waving as we drove away in our Dodge van!

Dr. Stewart was correct! Sometimes, we could get one of our little angels to go to sleep; however, the other little angel would start screaming and wake up her sister!

Our little girls wouldn't go to sleep with their last bottles until around 10:00 to 10:30 p.m. Sometimes one of the girls would vomit all the milk she had just taken as we were very quietly and slowly rocking them. The other precious angel would start crying and spitting up. So, then we would have to give them both another bath, a clean diaper and gown.

When the girls were six weeks old, I started my third year of teaching in my second county in North Florida. This time I would teach only children with a specific learning disability (SLD) in reading/written language or math skills. There were no crossover students at that time. The school I was hired to teach in, Shadeville Elementary in earlier days, had been where all the black children in the county attended K-12. This was before integration. So, it was an old school!

Every morning Jason and I drove twenty miles to our babysitter, Ms. Yvonne's new home. At the time, Yvonnes parents were living on her property in a motor home. Her mom and dad were there temporarily while her dad was undergoing treatment for a medical problem in Tallahassee.

After the first week of going to Ms. Yvonne's and her new home for five straight days, mornings and afternoons, I decided that something had to give! So, for a couple of months, Richard was able to change his schedule and would have Thursdays and Fridays off and work on Saturdays and Sundays. However, we'd still pay Yvonne and her mom the same amount weekly to hold our twins' places. The ladies would each take a baby and a diaper bag with formula ready to go, another outfit if needed, diapers, quilts, and toys.

Later in the evening, I could enjoy Richard and Jason, and I could spend time with the girls. Richard would usually start dinner on Thursdays and Fridays, and I would usually finish, and we both would clean the kitchen, and then both of us would give our little girls their nice warm baths and put them in their nightgowns. We read to Jason and helped him learn his sight word cards and asked him about first grade. It was new to him having baby sisters in the house.

Richard would take care of both of our little girls by himself during those two school days. Plus, he would wash and dry the clothes and have everything put away, clean the house, and usually have something started for dinner! So, when Jason and I got home, Richard was ready to go outside with our son and cut and stack wood for our new limestone fireplace or continue to work on Jason's tree house that they were building. Richard was wonderful!

As our little girls grew, they would usually start crying and sucking on their fingers or fists because they were hungry, again. I would have to be the one to come to their rescue and give them their last bottles, just around 6:00 to 6:30 a.m. before we left for Ms. Yvonne's house in the mornings! Jason and I could just listen to twin girls, each with a great set of lungs screaming. Not! By this time, Richard was back at work five straight days a week.

Then, after I got Jason and his bookbag in the car and buckled in, the girls' diaper bags and my school bag and briefcase in the car, it was time to put our sweet girls in the car and strap them in their car seats. At least once or twice a week, things didn't go as well as I had hoped. As I was trying to get everyone in their places with bright, shining faces, at least one of our little girls would spit up milk in my hair and on my clothes! So, I kept perfume and soap in my desk and would try to cover the "lovely odor of soured milk in the morning!"

When I arrived at Shadeville to see my room, I discovered that my room would be in the girls' old locker and dressing room in the gym. I was so disappointed. It was a dusty and musty smelling old place. The high windows were filthy, and the room had an ugly painted concrete floor, which had seen better days. There was a girl's bathroom with a door. The sinks, which were outside the bathroom, were terribly stained with mold, mildew, paint, and who knows what else?

Mr. Kittrell, the school foreman said they would paint the room a light cream, which would improve the walls immensely, and the floor was finally covered with dark red indoor-outdoor carpet! Mr. Smokey, the janitor, used strong chemicals and finally cleaned the sink after a couple of hours!

On the other side of the gym, the Emotional Behavioral disorders (EBO) class was housed in the former boy's dressing/locker room. They had a large bathroom, as well. At the end of my fourth year of teaching at Shadeville (six years in all), it looked like I would have to move to another school in Wakulla County. The problem was that we had low numbers of identified specific learning-disabled children, or SLD students!

Since I was certified in mental retardation and specific learning disabilities, from kindergarten through twelfth, I felt I could easily get another position. However, I didn't want to move to another school! I enjoyed my school and students in my classes, as well as the adults that I knew at Shadeville!

I spoke with my principal and the Wakulla County Special Education Administration. I asked if I could keep the students classified as mentally retarded, now mentally or intellectually disabled (MID or ID) in our school district as well.

Finally, it was decided that I could keep the Specific Learning Disabled (SLD) kids as well as the few Educable Mentally Disabled children!

It made sense; the kids wouldn't have to ride in the old county station wagon twice a day every day. They would instead just come to Shadeville Elementary and stay all day! They could now really feel a real part of our school!

So, now I would have two Exceptionalities in my class! After all, at my first school, Carrabelle, I had taught three exceptionalities!

Jenny was my first student with Down's Syndrome at Shadeville, and I loved her! She had a sweet family. Her mother was a nurse in Tallahassee at the hospital, and her father ran their family grocery store in a little community in Saint Marks.

Jenny's older sister was beautiful and brilliant and participated in the county Gifted program.

One day I went into the storeroom in the gym where outdated materials had been stacked in boxes and stored for years. As I was perusing the materials, I found some old simple books and workbooks for Special Education students. They were the "Mary, Bill, and King" book series for Educable Mentally Retarded students. Of course, now, there are updated and less distasteful terms for people with disabilities.

The characters in the book series were simply drawn; however, the books were in color and added a few more words in each book. Using a few sight words at first, and mainly using nouns and then adding verbs and some adjectives, the stories really worked for my sweet little girls!

Jenny had a best friend in my class who was named Kam. She had been born with Alcohol Syndrome and was close to the same age as Jenny.

They both loved everything we did in my class! When they finished a "Mary, Bill, and King" book, I always rewarded them with a brightly colored award. I would put their names on the awards, and then they could pick a prize out of my special prize box! They were both so appreciative of everything!

Kam's mother was an older woman and an alcoholic. So, poor Kam didn't have much of a chance to learn at home. Our school social worker told me that her mother's backyard was piled high with beer cans and wine bottles!!

Kammie, or Kam, was so sweet, so happy, and I called her my little butterfly because she would flit around my room checking out this and that, while "oohing and aahing." Kammie would usually wait for Jenny outside of Jenny's home room so they could hold hands while walking down the sidewalk into my classroom.

I helped the little girls make folders for their work, and they had a small alcove in my classroom where they kept their things. I would also write with bright markers on the low white board in their reading area. Then, they would both trace over the sentence in different colored markers as they read the sentence to each other. They loved it.

Kammie, especially, would squeal from happiness! They would also use colored markers to go over names and other words from their worksheets.

Several years later, Jenny and her family moved to Tallahassee when their oldest daughter was in middle school.

Jenny and her parents wrote me a sweet letter when Jenny graduated from Special education classes in high school in Tallahassee, Florida.

Jenny told me she could take the city bus by herself to a McDonald's restaurant where she was a French fry cook! When I read that, it was one of my proudest moments as a teacher!

I had started Jenny on her way! I had given her family hope that Jenny could succeed in her own time and in her own way. I wrote back to her and her family and reminded them of the Mary, Bill, and King books. I sent a nice card and a nice check! I still get tears when I think of that tiny little girl with the pixie haircut and her first years in my classroom!

While at Shadeville Elementary School, I had many students whom I will never forget!

Peggy was a pretty girl with long, beautiful red hair and pale, lightly freckled skin. When my fifth-grade group would talk about their families, Peggy would always seem very secretive and sad and would not join in the conversations in my room. Sometimes during a class lesson Peggy would just put her head down on her desk with tears in her eyes and not say a word. She mention that she and her younger brother, Thomas, lived in their old single wide trailer in an old park.

Since their mother worked nights at a local bar in the area, they usually stayed home by themselves. The family dynamic changed when their mother's jobless boyfriend moved in the already cramped living space and stayed in the mobile home with the kids at night while mom worked at the local bar.

Peggy was twelve years old and was rapidly maturing physically. For the talent show at our school that year, Peggy started dancing to music in a very provocative way that she had brought from home for the gym record player. Her homeroom teacher didn't think to check what kind of music it was. However, that was a big mistake! The music was something you might hear in a gentleman's club. All the classes seemed mesmerized as they watched her dance!

Peggy was wearing tight short shorts with her eyes closed. The principal and other teachers started looking at me to stop the dance, which was very risqué. However, I thought that it would be even worse to stop her dancing!

I had my suspicions that she was being sexually molested, probably by her mom's new boyfriend. So, after the talent show, I called our wonderful overworked social worker and asked her to start showing up at Peggy's mother's mobile home and to ask her to come in for a conference with her teachers.

After several trips to the mobile home without a response, our social worker sent a certified letter to ask for a meeting.

Since there was no answer about the meeting, and Peggy and her brother had both been absent from school for several days, I was worried!

So, our diligent social worker went back to the mobile home park office and found out that Peggy and her family—including her mom's unemployed boyfriend—had moved to Georgia!!

The local school system tried to find out where they were in Georgia but was unable to get any contact information, since they were now out of state. Of course, this was before cell phones and even computers were still very limited.

I still remember too many times, when Peggy came to my classroom, she seemed very sad, and sometimes she would be crying and would just put her head down on her desk. I have never forgotten poor Peggy and occasionally still wonder what really happened to her.

The guidance counselors always told me that they couldn't really bring up a touchy subject like sexual molestation without the student mentioning it first.

For several months, our female counselor was out of work because she had a heart valve torn when her doctor was trying to insert a camera down the artery. Her doctor was trying to take pictures of what might be going on to make her constantly have an irregular heartbeat. So, then our sweet counselor had to have surgery and get a new heart valve. After that, it was a long while before she was released to drive about an hour and a half to school.

Another female student that I had really worried about was Jeanette. I taught her in 4th, 5th, and 6th grade before the middle school was built. She had a specific learning disability in reading and written language skills. She was a pretty girl, quiet, shy, and very serious around most people.

Jeanette also had an older sister, Wanda, in fifth grade (one year ahead of Jeanette, but two years older than her). Wanda had deep seated emotional problems and was placed in the special needs class for the emotionally disturbed next door to my classroom in the old gym.

Wanda had major issues, she would constantly lie, steal, and commit bizarre' crimes around the school. She would cause damage in the hall bathrooms by clogging toilets with bathroom tissue and paper towels, and flushing the toilets, which would overflow, then she would do the same things to the bathroom sinks!

Wanda would also knock over large outdoor trash cans and kick the trash all over the ground. She would steal and throw things in the regular and special needs class and hit the kids in the back of their heads and lie about it.

An awful story that I remember about Wanda was when her special education teacher for emotional behavior disorders, or E/BD, couldn't find Wanda in her E/BD classroom. Her teacher looked behind cabinets, doors, in the bathroom, etc. She even looked in my room, but no Wanda to be seen! Finally, her teacher looked under a big table, and there she was—giving oral sex to a twelve-year-old boy with a smile on his face, as he was sitting at the big table!!

Wanda was seriously mentally ill and had no friends, except maybe that fifth grade boy! Of course, since Jeanette was her sister, a lot of students picked on her, as well. When she would go into her regular education class, she would usually find the contents of the classroom trash can poured all over her desk! If she forgot and left personal items in her desk while she went to my class, the items would either be stolen or broken when she went back!

I had talked to her regular education teacher about the kids stealing and/or breaking the few things she had. Miss Young said that she couldn't do anything about it because the kids would sneak around and would never admit who had grabbed her stuff! So, one day when Jeanette was absent, I asked to talk to Miss Young's class.

Jeanette was very quiet and timid. She would not hurt anyone in anyway.

Jeanette had no friends because of her bizarre sister's behaviors! Of course, since Jeanette was Wanda's younger sister, most kids tried to bully her and make fun of her, as well!

I thought at least when Wanda went to middle school the following year and Jeanette was in fifth grade, maybe the terrible stories about her sister would die down.

However, when Jeanette went to fifth grade, the terrible things continued to plague her! So, I met with the fourth and fifth grade teachers and asked them to please talk to their classes and try to be kind to Jeanette. It wasn't her fault that her sister had such awful behaviors! Things weren't always great for Jeanette, but since her sister wasn't around our school anymore, a lot of the meanness died down.

Poor Jeanette still couldn't seem to have a normal life! One day, after school at Shadeville, I was surprised to see Jeanette walk through my classroom door! I hadn't seen her in a couple of years!

By this time, she was very pretty and mature and at the local middle school in eighth grade. She had long, reddish blond hair and pretty skin. I was happy to see her, but I was upset about what she told me!

Jeanette's bizarre parents had two old mobile homes on their property, and they were placed in an "L" shape. Her parents were renting out a bedroom in one of the trailers to an older man. However, that wasn't all. That guy was trying to sneak into Jeanette's room at night and wanted to have sex with her! I believed that she was telling me the truth! She had never lied to me before, and she was shaking with tears in her eyes, and I could tell that she was really scared!

I promised I would call someone for her, and I did, our school social worker. Our social worker told me that she would go out to their place and discuss what Jeanette had said to me. However, after talking to Jeanette's parents, our social worker said that she thought that Jeanette had made up the story!

I never believed that Jeanette had gone to that much trouble to make up a story just so she could come and see me. It didn't make sense. First, Jeanette had to talk to the bus driver that knew her family and let her hitch a ride to Shadeville Elementary and then have the bus driver wait while Jeanette talked to me. Then the bus driver would have to drive to Jeanette's family's home.

I didn't believe that she was lying to me, but I was told she wasn't my student anymore and I couldn't do anything else to help her. I never saw Jeanette again because I was told that she was not my responsibility anymore, and she never came back to see me again. I always felt like I had failed her in some way. As a reminder of her, I always kept an empty folder with her name on it in my file cabinet where my students' files were kept at school. I took that empty file folder with me to every school in which I ever taught, as a reminder of that poor girl—when I couldn't help her.

Now, since I have retired, I keep the empty folder with her name on it in my home office!

Occasionally, I still think about certain students that I tried to help over my thirty-five years career of teaching the neediest.

Another child I think about is Maria, a sweet little girl who was eight years old with long blond hair and big blue eyes. Our school secretary called on the intercom that Maria's father (who was the "noncustodial" parent) was on the way to my room to pick her up early.

Her father had a letter that he had shown to the school secretary and then to me. As the father and sweet, beautiful little Maria walked out of my room for the last time, I called the office and told the secretary that I was worried! Maria didn't seem to know anything about her father coming to pick her up!

Our fabulous school secretary finally got in touch with Maria's mom, and she called the police! However, Maria and her dad were gone from the school parking lot, and I never saw that sweet little girl again! I was told I had done the right thing, and so had our secretary. However, I still felt terrible! I never heard anything else about beautiful, sweet little Maria!

I also had a twelve-year-old girl, named Alice, from another county in Florida who had recently been adopted by a professional older couple. Her new parents seemed very concerned. The couple worked in Tallahassee but lived in Wakulla County. Alice rode the school bus to a friend's house and did her homework while waiting for her newly adoptive parents to come pick her up.

Alice's adoptive mother wore a very short and simple haircut, plus she was heavy and usually wore pant suits and no makeup. Mrs. Blake, Alice's adoptive mother, was not a very feminine woman; however, she had a good heart and wanted to make a happy life for their new twelve-year-old daughter. She talked with me several times about her new daughter starting to wet her bed most nights. She even stopped me on the road to talk, before they picked up their daughter at her friend's house.

Alice's new mom sent me notes telling me that she was at her wits end! Alice had been to specialists and was given meds for the bedwetting, but nothing helped! Alice's mom would wake up during the night and make her daughter go to the bathroom a couple of times a night. Alice always said she was sorry and acted ashamed that she wet the bed again.

In the morning, she would usually have wet sheets and blankets! We discussed having her change her own sheets, nothing to drink after dinner, etc. However, nothing changed!

I always suspected the adoptive father was molesting her or tried to, and this was a way of keeping him out of her bed. However, I had no evidence. Her adoptive father seemed "very stoic" and not very friendly or talkative.

I spoke with our guidance counselor about this, troubled girl several times; however, she couldn't do much because Alice wouldn't bring up the subject.

Our guidance counselor was a lovely woman, and so was her daughter, who had graduated from Florida State University, with a degree in theater arts. She appeared in several movies and played a major role in a CBS comedy series in the late 1980's based in Miami, Florida. She even wore a Florida State University T-shirt on some of the shows!

Then, almost before I knew it, the school year was over, and Alice would be going to Wakulla Middle School! I put a note in her special education folder that I was worried about her and hoped her mother could get to the root of the problem, before anything or anyone physically hurt her. I also put my personal phone number in her folder.

An even worse story was that another one of my students—Mary's father was also her grandfather! The grandfather had molested his own daughter, and his daughter became pregnant with beautiful little Mary!

Then his daughter gave birth to a little girl who was later found to have a specific learning disability. When I asked what happened to the grandfather/father, I found out that things were kept quiet in the small backwoods community where they lived! Most of my students were poor and really didn't seem to know that they lived in poverty because most of their friends did too!

One time, two brothers who were in my classroom at different times during the school day for a specific learning disability came into my room early before school to tell me a funny story. The funny part had happened over the weekend!

The brothers had spent the night at Danny's house, also a student in my classroom. They were laughing so hard that they could barely stand up! However, they finally found the wherewithal to stop laughing and tell me the story of the rat that got under the bottom sheet in the bed that all three boys were supposed to be sleeping in! They felt a lump moving under the sheets and decided to beat and kick the lump to death! They were demonstrating on the floor how they killed the rat and explained to me how gruesome it had been. They told me blood splattered everywhere! When I asked the brothers where they slept for the night they said in unison, "in the same bed!" They said they all just kicked the "lump" to the bottom of the bed and just laughed about it!

Just then, Danny came into my classroom and wanted to talk about the poor rat that the boys killed over the weekend, as well!

I just laughed with them. I would have probably been up all night looking around for monster mice! If a mouse had even gotten into my house, much less my bed, I would probably have run outside and slept in my car!

Another story about one of my students, Bobby. He came from a very poor family.

When any student in my classroom had a birthday, I would always give them a birthday card and trip to the prize box. The next day kids would ask what they got for their birthday from their parents. Bobby was proud of his gift—his own box of some type of cereal!

The students thought he was joking at first and started laughing. However, it was true, and I could see that he was embarrassed. I told the class that I would love to have my favorite box of cereal for my own birthday, too!! Then, I asked every student in the classroom what their favorite cereal was and helped to deflect the issue. Then, we all got back to work.

I had figured out that Bobby's mother was a working woman in the sex trade. Bobby had told me that his mother had many different "boyfriends," sometimes several in one evening. It was easy to get into the house—there was no door.

Our social worker had been there several times because Bobby's mother had several young teenage daughters that the social worker was worried about. However, I was also worried about Bobby!

Bobby told me privately that he would try to get out of the house early before his mom's "gentlemen friends" started coming by in the evening.

If he made it out in time, he said he would usually sleep in a wild blackberry patch or under their unpainted wooden shack. If he got to the blackberry patch, he would usually have thorns from the blackberry bushes in his dark chocolate skin the next day.

Sometimes I would send Bobby to the front office to see the school secretary, who would use tweezers to get the stickers from the blackberry bushes out of his skin. She would apply some medicated cream to soothe his skin.

Mrs. Tripp was wonderful! We did not have school nurses in the school system in Wakulla County in those days, so we were glad to have Mrs. Tripp help with cough drops, Band-Aids, etc.

One day, poor Bobby said his bottom really hurt, and he could barely walk or sit down! I suspected that he didn't get out of his house quickly enough, and he had probably been molested by one of his mother's customers! I called our social worker, and she came to our classroom and took Bobby for a walk outside. Mrs. Moore talked with him, but he never admitted that someone had raped him. We all suspected that was what had happened to him! Probably, his mother told him not to say anything, and he never did! However, he did walk very gingerly and carefully sit down for a week or more!

Another notable student, Robert, had Tourette's syndrome. He was a fifth grader and often licked the cream-colored walls in my classroom. Robert would sometimes try to swallow long pieces of yarn.

Robert had normal intelligence and was on medication; however, it was still difficult to get him to focus on his work. He loved to draw and was talented. Every time a rocket was about to lift off from Cape Kennedy (in 1986) now, it has changed back to the original name, Cape Canaveral on the east coast of Florida—our principal would announce it. Mr. Maxwell would tell everyone to turn on their televisions in their classrooms and watch history being made! It was always exciting, and we would stop what we were doing—as a school—and watch the count down and liftoff! We could always hear the entire school cheering!

This time, in 1986, it was going to really be exciting because Christa McAuliffe, a teacher from New Hampshire, had applied and won the coveted spot as the payload specialist. She was going to conduct experiments on the trip into space, and they were going to be broadcast on television for all the schoolchildren in America!

We were all watching and holding our collective breath, and then the unthinkable happened! After the rocket lifted off the pad at Cape Canaveral, the rocket containing the seven astronauts, including teacher Christa McAuliffe, exploded!

Soon, Mr. Maxwell, our principal, asked everyone to please turn off all the televisions in the school!

Christa McAuliffe had become a superstar to thousands of schoolchildren who were going to get to watch her conduct experiments in space!

Christa McAuliffe had become one of more than 11,000 educators who applied to be part of NASA's new "Teacher in Space Project." On July 1, 1985, it was announced Christa had been chosen as one of the ten finalists, and in July, she traveled to Johnson Space Center for a week of thorough medical exams and briefings about space flight.

Christa McAuliffe was to be part of the Space Shuttle mission, and Barbara Morgan was her backup if Christa could not go or changed her mind.

Both teachers each took a yearlong leave of absence from teaching to train for a Space Shuttle mission in early 1986. NASA paid both of their salaries. McAuliffe would conduct experiments and teach lessons from space. The lessons were to be broadcast to millions of school children via closed circuit TV. To record her thoughts, Christa intended to keep a personal journal like a "woman on the Conestoga wagons pioneering in the West."

On January 28, 1986, Christa McAuliffe boarded Challenger with the other six crew members of STS-51-L.

Seventy-three seconds into the flight at an altitude of 48,000 feet, the shuttle broke apart, resulting in the deaths of all seven crew members.

According to NASA, it was in part because of the excitement over Christa McAuliffe's presence on the space shuttle that the terrible accident had such a significant impact on our nation. Many children in the United States were watching the live launch, and media coverage was extensive of the accident.

When our principal realized something terribly wrong had happened, he announced that all televisions in the school should be turned off immediately. The next week all Robert, my 5th grade student with Tourette's syndrome, could think about was Christa McAuliffe and the other astronauts that "were blown to pieces" and "the fire and the pieces of the rocket that rained down." Robert loved to draw, and he was very talented in art and couldn't focus on anything else, at this time, and kept interrupting me while I was trying to teach groups.

Then, I hit on an idea and called his mother to let her know that I was going to give Robert a special assignment. Robert already knew all the names of the six crew members killed on Challenger, and that was all, he could focus on and think about. I told him to draw each astronaut and write their name under their picture. His mother gave me her best wishes!

I bought Robert a good quality sketch pad and brought in a recent newspaper that had photos of everyone who had died in the tragedy. This quieted Robert, and he worked diligently at his assignment. He wanted everything just right. When he finished, I told him that I would bring in a nice box and we would put all the portraits that he had drawn, each with their names in the box.

We would have a small funeral service complete with the eulogy given by our understanding principal, Mr. Maxwell. Finally, the box with the portraits of everyone who had died in the disaster would be laid to rest. After the burial, there could be no more discussion about the astronauts. We would have to let them go.

We had a small funeral in an area near the playground complete with a burial. There could be no more talking about the astronauts and how they had died. We were all properly quiet and solemn. Robert was finally able to close this terrible and shocking chapter in his life. He was able to get back to learning again!

Most of the students at Shadeville Elementary School lived on unpaved roads, as did most of the other kids in the county. If it started raining heavily, it might be impossible to get the kids riding buses home safely. Occasionally, the school day would have to be shortened. The buses could drop the kids off early and make it down the muddy roads before they flooded.

One day I received a parental note from a poor woman with three or four young children—one of which was in my classroom part time. She detailed in her note that she had driven down a dirt road while it was raining, and the car had gotten stuck up to the bumpers!

They all got out of the car and into the muddy road and attempted to push it out of the mud! They were unable to budge the car! The mom and her three young children had to spend the night in the car in the middle of the muddy mess on the forest road!

There were no sidewalks or streetlights to comfort them. Remember, there were no cell phones in those days! There were only the sounds of owls, bats, foxes, wolves, and other wild animals scampering around for food! The mother kept hoping someone with a big truck would come down the road; no one did that night! Finally, the next morning, a man in a truck came down the muddy dirt road and pulled the car out.

All was not well; the car lost its front bumper while it was being freed from the mud. That was why her daughter didn't get her homework done the night before! (Of course, I excused her daughter's homework!!)

It wasn't hard to believe her story. School days were often shortened or would start later in the day if it was during the raining season; buses would be unable to get down the many dirt roads that would flood close to the rivers or low swampy land, even if there were ditches to help drain the dirt roads.

Finally, summer break arrived. My son, Jason, answered the house phone (before cell phones) one weekend and seemed upset. When he hung up, he told me that one of my students, Steven, who would be in middle school in the fall, had been killed while riding his four-wheeler!

He according to the information, was hit by a log truck.

We called around and couldn't confirm if it was true.

I never could get anyone on the phone who knew anything about a wreck that weekend. It was a beautiful summer weekend. Most families were probably fishing, scalloping, pulling crab traps, swimming, boating, or just enjoying the day. Finally, we found out that it was just a cruel joke!

The story doesn't end there! By the end of summer break, a couple of months later, when school was back in session, I saw Steven at the new middle school. I was there to pick up my son, Jason, for a dentist's appointment. While I was waiting for my son, Steven saw me, smiled, and came over to talk. He looked good, had a nice haircut, and had on a familiar light blue pullover shirt with a collar and jeans.

Steven talked about how happy he was in middle school; he said that he really liked all his teachers and still loved riding his four-wheeler. I asked him to please be careful, and he told me he always was! Soon, Jason came to my car, and we drove away.

On the way to Jason's dental appointment, we laughed and even got angry about those wild twin boys who had told a terrible lie about Steven being killed on his four-wheeler during the summer. However, we tried to laugh it off!

Then, a couple of days later he was killed while riding on his four-wheeler and was gone forever!

My husband and I attended the funeral of a twelve-year-old! I sent his mother a card with a letter enclosed, written from my heart. He had been in my class for three years and was always very easy going! He usually had a big smile when he came into my classroom. Also, he was a friend of my son, Jason.

A couple of weeks later, a mother showed up at Shadeville's front office, crying and asking to see me! The school secretary called and told me that she was sending an angry and distraught parent to my room! I searched my mind to try and figure out what I had done or said to a child to make her so upset. I didn't know who was coming; our secretary didn't think to ask her name.

I was surprised but glad to see Steven's mom. She told me what I had written on my card to her and her family. This note she said eased her pain and gave her hope. He died doing what he loved, riding his four-wheeler out in the woods and countryside! Then we both hugged and cried!

Several years before we moved from Wakulla County to Leon County, Florida, the state of Florida devised a long evaluation instrument to determine if a teacher was really a master teacher.

The teachers who applied would also be observed teaching in their classrooms several times by at least two different evaluators.

Lesson plans would be checked to see if they were being followed so that the students could meet the grade level standards. The appropriate use of materials was checked.

Finally, teachers in our county, as well as teachers in every county in Florida, were required to take a long-written examination at a designated place. The exam would help determine if the teachers could follow the state standards for their subjects and grade levels they were hired to teach.

The Exceptional Education or Special Education teachers, had to know the criteria for placement in exceptional student classrooms.

The ESE, or exceptional student education teachers, would need to know how to write individual education plans (IEPs) for each student in their class. As I waited in line for the State Education Building to open in Tallahassee, I saw a number of teachers from other schools in our county.

When I asked a few teachers if they had studied the regulations of exceptional student criteria, most said, "No, you either know it or you don't."

I always liked to be prepared, so I studied for several weeks. I always liked to have a high comfort level from rereading things that I already knew and trying my best.

Later, when our test scores were finally sent out from, only two teachers made it from Shadeville Elementary, a good friend of ours and me! Our names were printed in the newspaper!

I'm sure there were many other deserving teachers at Shadeville Elementary. However, they had been too confident and didn't study or study enough.

That meant that we were rewarded for excellent knowledge and teaching skills in our areas! The best part was, in those days, since teachers didn't get paid in the summer, most needed to save ahead for a nice vacation, and now we didn't have worries!

For three years, every summer, the teachers who had been the first to receive the $9,000 bonus, would be sent $3,000 extra in the summer!

The second year, if the teachers passed the requirements, they would only receive a total of $1500 for one year! Then the program fizzled out!

I wanted to complete my master's degree in reading/English education through high school. I continued to teach during the day and drove to Florida State University after school. I attended two nights a week during the school year and three days a week one summer. Since I had two college interns—different times of the school year—I was surprised to open a letter from

Florida State University one day. Florida State Teachers' College sent me two certificates, each for a free semester of all the classes I wanted to take to finish my master's degree. Those certificates were worth thousands of dollars! I would have a nice pay raise when I finished the classes. To attend FSU during the week, we would have to meet Daddy on the side of the road, coming from Tallahassee where he was now working. We switched the girls and the car seats and then our son, Jason to Richard's vehicle. Richard continued home to make sure all had baths and dinner. He also helped Jason with homework.

    I came in late at night and rushed to bed and started over the next day! It was difficult, but Richard and I worked together to accomplish another goal for our family.

    With another degree from Florida State, I would hopefully become a better teacher and of course have a larger income for our growing family.

    I had a few parents that stayed in touch with me over the years. Some would send a note or just call me. Some would even knock on my classroom door before or after school if they were concerned about something. Several parents wanted their children to have some meaningful homework several times a week. So, I would have my paraprofessional copy some short stories from some of my own teacher's materials for them. If their child was in my class for math, I would have extra worksheets for them to practice on. Then weekly the homework would be sent home to complete. On Fridays they could earn extra points for a nice prize. Most families didn't ask for extra work for their child; however, the ones that did got plenty.

George's mom would usually call me at least once or twice a week, and we became close over the four years that George was in my class. George was a good kid but could be devious. George's mom knew that and would call me if she didn't hear back from me by phone or note.

Sometimes he would "forget" to return a note or "lose it." I had sent extra work home with him. He usually returned at least one page to me every day. His mom wanted him to have meaningful activities to complete instead of just watching television every night.

Whenever he wouldn't finish his class assignments, I would also send them home with him to complete and return.

However, George told his mom a little story; he said that he didn't have any homework for that whole week! George's mom called me at school to find out for sure.

I told her that George was mistaken. He did have some homework because he wasn't finishing classroom assignments! He hadn't returned a few pages of reading vocabulary and comprehension questions.

George's mom was determined that he was not going to get away with lying to her! She looked all over his bedroom and couldn't find any work that he had hidden from her. So, she hunted in the garage for his work—nothing! Then she decided to go out to his swing set and old sandbox that he liked to build roads and towns in for his matchbox cars. There was a nice-looking hill he had made and "lo and behold" she discovered the missing homework buried under the hill.

Mrs. Howard was so aggravated by her son's deceitful behaviors that she put all the work in a bag, even though some of it was damp and mildewed.

She drove to my classroom, parked right outside the gym where my room was housed. Poor George! Mrs. Howard dumped the incomplete work on his desk. Then she told George to tell me where he had hidden it! All color left George's face as his mom took him by his hand while holding a paddle and walked him to our in-class bathroom!

My whole class was stunned, and not a sound was made by any of my students—at their desks—when George was given a spanking by his mother! I always had compassion for my special needs students and their families!

George's mom was no exception. He was an only child. George had been born with a cleft palate, which had been repaired before he had started school, but he still needed speech therapy.

He received speech therapy at Shadeville, as well as special education services from my classroom.

When George finished fifth grade, his parents sent a very complimentary letter to our Superintendent of Wakulla County Schools about Shadeville Elementary School and all the teachers that had taught George over the six years (K-5th grade) he attended.

Later, when George graduated from high school, his parents invited me to attend his graduation ceremony. At the time we were living in Washington state and didn't get the invitation until after graduation had passed.

I sent George and his parents a nice card with a letter and a check for George. I was so proud of him and his family. They had supported George and his teachers all through his school career.

George's parents wrote another kind letter to me. They gave me so much credit for teaching the educational building blocks to help him throughout his school career.

I didn't deserve all the credit; his parents always stood by him, and there were staff members that helped him so much and gave him confidence.

Even our two custodians, Mr. Smokey, who was a sweet old guy, who liked to smoke a cigar at lunch every day—on top of part of the gym—and Mr. Kitrell, who was the guy that everybody turned to for difficult issues. Mr. Kitrell always wore a pressed and lightly starched khaki shirt and pressed pants!

Teachers would go to these men and they would build nice new bookcases, shelves, tables, and repair items the best they could. Sometimes, if George was having a bad day, I would send a note to Mr. Kitrell asking that George could help him for a while, maybe for twenty minutes or so. When he came back to class, he usually came back with a better attitude.

Even though Wakulla County was poor, most people had jobs. Many people worked in the forestry industries or seafood industry. Some drove to Tallahassee to work. They did the best they could for their families.

Most parents came to parent-teacher meetings and other activities the schools sponsored. Shadeville Elementary was known for a great Halloween carnival. The main money makers were the prince and princess from each grade level. It was really a simple concept. One boy and one girl from each homeroom were picked. Each child that was picked would put a picture of themselves on several jars. Usually, photos would be photocopied and taped to jelly jars, pickle jars, or baby food jars.

The fifth grade students with the most money in their jars would be crowned King and Queen of the Halloween Carnival. (Every penny was a vote, so every dollar was worth one hundred votes!) Plus, the top moneymakers in each of the lower grades would be the princes and princesses!

The jars were placed in stores, shops, banks, offices, and gas stations anywhere people could see the jars with photos and drop a few coins in. The jars were even taken to work by their parents.

Even then, I was surprised about how much money was raised for our school! Shadeville Elementary always raised several thousand dollars through the King and Queen of the Halloween Carnival!

The three most popular and biggest money-making activities were Bingo, Haunted

House, and the Hayride (a hay wagon pulled by a tractor). Richard, my husband was usually the tractor driver, and he loved it! Early in the day, I would have already put ghosts in the trees, a few witches, and a couple of skeletons for good measure! Then I would get into the back of the hay wagon dressed as some crazy witch with a flashlight that I could shine on "terrible creatures!" Of course, all the girls would usually scream in good fun!

I had received a call from the secretary at Shadeville School. She informed me our principal had received a call from a parent with two children who would be new part time students in my special education classes. The mother of those students wanted to meet with me before the school year started.

We drove about 20 minutes to Shadeville Elementary School's office. When we got to school, I gave Jason my room key and had him take Adrien and Arien, our twin girls, to my room. Then I told him, "Don't let anyone else in my classroom!"

The principal informed the mother about my education and experience in the special education field as we walked and chatted to my classroom. When I got to the door, Arien pushed it open to tell me that Adrien's finger had been cut off!

Yes, part of her wedding ring finger had certainly been cut off! Our principal turned pale, and I know I did!

We were still standing in the hall, peering into the classroom. We saw Jason washing Adrien's left hand as she whimpered. I saw her fingertip was now square cut, and there didn't seem to be any fingernail left! You could see the bloody white bone of her sweet little finger! The rest of her finger and hand seemed intact. Remember, our twins would turn five just before kindergarten started.

We were all in shock! I remember saying, "I can't believe I'm looking for my daughter's finger! Our principal ran back to the office to call for an ambulance because Adrien had turned ghostly pale but was not talking or crying! She was just standing there, going into shock!

I found the missing piece of Adrien's finger in the hallway, outside of my door!

We put the part of the finger in a cup of ice. When we got back to the office, the ambulance was waiting.

A teacher and friend of mine invited Jason and Arien to go home with her and her two kids when she left school that day.

Meanwhile, I called my husband, Richard, about the incident, and he met us at the hospital in Tallahassee.

Adrien and I were transported by ambulance from Crawfordville to Tallahassee, and she never made a sound! She had an oxygen mask on and was deathly pale! The EMT said that Adrien was in shock!

That is until her daddy—whom I had called from school earlier—met us at the emergency room entrance.

Then Adrien uttered her first word since the incident, "Daddy!" Then they were both crying as he grabbed her into his arms.

A well-known hand specialist reattached Adrien's fingertip at the hospital. The end of her third finger died even with medications and a special cast! Later, our doctor was able to sew her third finger from her left hand to her palm, in hopes that the operation would work. She would have to wear a full arm brace for four to six weeks. I think, it was harder for us, her parents, than it was for Adrien!

The difficult part of the entire ordeal, was trying to keep her from running, jumping, and climbing trees, so that she wouldn't rip out the delicate stitches!

Later our doctor finally removed the brace and cut the finger skin that had grown to the palm of her hand. Then he reattached a lid to the top of her third finger on her left hand! Our doctor was also able to save a little piece of nail bed, and now it looks great! No one ever notices that her third finger is a little shorter!

After I finished another year at Shadeville Elementary, I started interviewing with principals in Tallahassee. It made sense because we had sold our home in Crawfordville, Florida, in anticipation of my husband, Richard, being hired by a federal agency. We had thought that he would have been picked quickly for a Federal Agent position in Alaska.

However, the Gramm Rudman Bill was pushed through by the Federal Government and there was a stop on new hiring in most agencies.

We bought a nice lot in a great Tallahassee neighborhood and built a new home. It would be hard to leave Shadeville Elementary where I had taught for eight years! Jason had started kindergarten at Shadeville and graduated from Shadeville! Also, he had only one more year of middle school to complete before he went to high school in ninth grade.

Adrien and Arien had started kindergarten at Shadeville Elementary and had completed second grade. I loved the people at Shadeville; however, it was about an hour and a half drive from the new home in Tallahassee.

I applied to schools in Tallahassee, and I was hired at Sabal Palm Elementary, which would only be a twenty-minute drive from the new place.

Since I intended to complete my Specialist Degree in Education in the evenings, it would be a shorter drive to Florida State University.

Afterword 1
Shadeville Elementary School, Wakulla County, Florida

After a lot of tears—mainly mine—Adrien's finger and left hand now looked great! She is left-handed! Lefties usually have an easier time writing with their right hand than righties who injure their right hand do, because lefties also must live in a basically right- handed world!

Afterward 2

Today, Wakulla County has modern schools and more schools than ever. There is still only one high school in the county: Wakulla High School. It has been updated with new baseball fields, a new football stadium, and a new track.

There are now two middle schools with nice sports facilities:

- Wakulla Middle School
- River Springs Middle School

The biggest changes are in the elementary schools. There are now four elementary schools—all built after we left the area:
- Medart Elementary School
- Shadeville Elementary School
- River Sink Elementary School
- Crawfordville Elementary School

Another change is that there is now a Wakulla County pre-kindergarten. It is housed in part of the old Shadeville Elementary where I taught many years ago.

The old Crawfordville Elementary has been repurposed as the Wakulla County School Board offices.

Chapter 3
Foreword

Sabal Palm Elementary Leon County, Florida

Tallahassee, Florida's history, which is also Leon County's history, began with the Native American population and their interactions with the British and Spanish colonists.

With early colonial Americans, who planted cotton on growing plantations, the area prospered so quickly that it became a city and the capital of Florida in 1821.

The name "Tallahassee" is a Native American word that translates as "old fields or town." This probably came from the Creek Indians (later called Seminoles) that migrated into the region in the 18th century.

Missionaries sent to the area from Spain intended to obtain food and cheap labor for the colony at St. Augustine. One of the most important mission sites, Mission San Luis de Apalachee, has been deemed a state historic site in Tallahassee.

The founding of Tallahassee was mainly a matter of convenience. In 1821, Florida was ceded by Spain to the United States. Tallahassee roughly lies midway between Pensacola and St. Augustine—the two largest cities in Florida at that time—which led the governor of the territories, William Pope Duval, to establish a commission to find a more central meeting place.

The commission chose the former Indian settlement of Tallahassee—fairly midway between the two cities, plus it was an area near the old capital of the Apalachee Chiefdom!

The rough log frontier capital building area gradually grew into a small town. In anticipation of becoming a state, the territorial government erected a Greek revival masonry building that looked more like a state Capitol. It opened in 1845 before statehood and eventually became known as the "old Capitol." It was later updated in the 1980s with new bright white paint and red and white striped awnings. It stands in front of the current capitol high rise today at the top of one of the seven hills that the city of Tallahassee is built on.

During the Civil War, Tallahassee was the only Confederate state capital east of the Mississippi River not captured by Union forces. The Battle of Natural Bridge was fought outside Tallahassee mostly by students of what would later become Florida State University, which is the only non-military academy or service academy school to have such a claim!

In 1883, Tallahassee carried out a state mandate requiring a state university. Classes were first held in the West Florida Seminary. Later, the state legislature changed the name to The Florida Military and Collegiate Institute to reflect the addition of a military action which trained male cadets. The university part of the school was called the Florida State College for Women.

However, in 1947 the governor of the state of Florida changed the name of the college to Florida State University, and it became a school of higher learning for men and women.

On October 3, 1887, The State Normal College for "Colored Students" opened its doors. It was not an official institution of higher learning until 1905 when the Buckman Act created the foundation for the modern Florida A&M University, which many men and women attend each year. Florida Agricultural and Mechanical University is now fully integrated as well.

During the last few years, there have been a multitude of comments and arguments about college and professional team names, especially when it comes to Native Americans. Some have felt it is degrading. So, teams have been pressured to change their names to make sure no one feels discriminated against.

However, the Seminole Tribunal Council did not want Florida State University to change the name of the FSU college mascot. They said they were honored that Florida State University still wanted to be known as a proud and strong tribe of Seminole warriors!

Sabal Palm Elementary School, Leon County, Florida

After I completed my seventh year of teaching special needs students in Wakulla County and my first two years in Franklin County (nine years in all), we sold our home in Crawfordville. We were still hoping that Richard would be hired by the federal government.

We had met a contractor and liked his model homes that he built in Tallahassee. So, we decided to have the contractor build a home for us. We had enjoyed our time in Wakulla County, but it was a long way for me to commute to Florida State University and back several nights a week. It was difficult on all of us!

So, it was wonderful when our new home in Tallahassee was completed! We had bought property in a beautiful neighborhood in the rolling red clay hills of north Tallahassee called Killearn Lakes Plantation.

We were blessed with beautiful old oaks, pines, wild roses, magnolias, and many other trees and bushes and several lakes. In the late evenings, lots of deer would come out to feed and bed down in our flower beds and newly sodded lawn.

For a while, we had a beautiful male peacock who was very tame and would strut around our acre of land. He was a bonus because he just showed up one day at our new home! Since we were in the back part of the neighborhood, we didn't have any neighbors. Pete, the peacock, would come into our garage if a garage door was open and peer into my back chrome bumper and peck at his reflection. I was afraid that he would jump up onto my new car and scratch the paint! I had just bought a new Cutlass Cierra Oldsmobile, and it was the "Seminole Edition" painted garnet (a dark red color) with two thin gold stripes along each side under the windows in the doors. (Remember we lived in "Seminole Country"!)

Sometimes we would feed "Pete" breadcrumbs, or dry dog food and bird seeds. "Pete" became accustomed to being fed by our three kids and would roost in one of our tall trees at night!

If our Boston terrier, Buster came out and saw the peacock, then a huge ruckus would ensue! The poor peacock would scream, screech, and fly up into a tree early in the afternoon and would not come down all night. Pete the Peacock lived with us for several months! The kids and I hoped he would come back; however, we never saw him again. I told the kids that he may have gone back to his other home before he came to visit us. We never did find any signs of beautiful peacock feathers on our property. So, we remained hopeful that he just decided to travel on…

Moving day had been amazing! We had lots of friends who lived in Tallahassee with trucks to help us move. They all went down to Crawfordville in Wakulla County and helped Richard load and carry our possessions back to Tallahassee. They even helped unload and place the furniture. Such great friends and busy times! Over the weekend we at least had our basic furniture in place and boxes in the correct rooms (most of the time!)

Of course, our pets were exploring the new house. Our black cat, Amos, who was Jason's age, thirteen years old, was also inside and outside exploring our new property. Jason walked around the house with Chris, his green parakeet, sitting on his shoulder. Jason also had a guinea pig, who had a nice house that my talented brother, Louis Wayne Novak, built on the edge of our new deck. Two hamsters named Zig and Zag that belonged to Adrien and Arien had a new home as well. Believe me, they were zigging and zagging in their nice cage and spinning their wheel.

Our new home was conveniently located near great shopping areas, Florida State University, doctors' offices, and our new Catholic Church (The Good Shepherd), where Jason was an altar boy. Jason also took a course in first aid so he could get paid for babysitting not only during some of the masses but also for some families in our new neighborhood.

I was so thrilled to live in such a beautiful area and hoped to finish my master's degree and then become a teaching assistant for Dr. Hafner at Florida State. Then I would start my specialist degree in reading and English. That would be wonderful since my professional goal was to become a professor at Florida State University.

We loved Tallahassee for many reasons! There were miles of oak canopy roads dripping with beautiful flowering vines and moss, lots of freshwater lakes, and rolling pastureland in the part of Tallahassee where we now lived. We had bought an acre of land in the back of Killearn Lakes Plantation on the circular street where it was quieter and safer when the kids were riding their bikes. We were in the last house in that part of the neighborhood.

All three of our children loved the area. We were about a block away from a pretty lake with a small island in the middle. It was aptly named "Lake Monkey Business"!

Every year the neighborhood would have fishing tournaments at Lake Monkey Business and have beautiful fireworks displays on the Fourth of July from that little island in the middle of the lake. Our family, and many of our neighbors in the area would walk or bike down to the lake and have picnics, "catch and release fish tournaments," etc. It was always fun, and adults and kids could win nice prizes. Arien, one of our twin girls, even won a nice rod and reel one time!

Since we lived about a block from the lake, our son Jason would go fishing often with friends or by himself. Richard had promised Jason that if he caught a "nice sized" bass, he would get it mounted for him. A few days later, Jason came home with a beautiful bass! He was so excited, grinning from ear to ear! The rod was even pulled out of his hand; however, he was able to grab the bass in the shallow water! Jason said he felt bad about it later, but the pretty bass died! We even took pictures of him and his fish. I felt bad for the fish, but we got it mounted anyway and hung it in his bedroom everywhere we lived.

I had interviewed with several principals in Tallahassee, and on my birthday, July 18, I was hired to teach students with specific learning disabilities at the elementary level and at my favorite school in Tallahassee, Sabal Palm Elementary. I was so thrilled! I had loved Shadeville Elementary and the people there in Wakulla County, but we had moved to Tallahassee, and I needed to stay close to Florida State University to continue my career goals.

Another plus was when I walked into the office at Sabal Palm Elementary, I saw a friend from my fifth and sixth grade elementary school years in the Tampa, Florida area! She had gotten married and now had two boys. Linda was the school secretary, and her husband had been assistant superintendent of Leon County (Tallahassee) schools in the past and was now running for head superintendent (it was an elected position).

I knew I would miss my friends at Shadeville Elementary, but we could talk on the phone and occasionally go back for special events, like the famous Halloween Carnival in Wakulla County, and let our children spend the night on weekends.

It was so much easier to drive to FSU when I lived in Tallahassee, and I quickly completed my master's degree in special education and reading and writing skills.

I was planning to start my specialist degree in reading and English skills through high school level the next year. In addition, my favorite professor at FSU had asked me to be his teaching assistant that coming year at FSU!

I was so excited that my dreams were coming true! In the meantime, in the back of our mind, we were still hoping that he would be hired by a Federal Law Enforcement agency—maybe locally—and not have to move again, unless it was moving to Alaska. I now had my master's degree certificates from Florida and Alaska. I had been offered a couple of teaching positions in Alaska, complete with a house, free electricity and fuel oil, plus free float plane flights to and from small schools on Native reservations. All I would have to do was drive a short distance to the float plane docks, and I would be flown to my school, and after school, I would be flown back to the docks and drive home. I would be making more money than a teacher with a doctorate degree in Florida was making! I was excited; it would be a great opportunity for our family. However, there was one problem; Richard would need to be hired by a Federal Law Enforcement Agency and take all the classes and go through all the training in Brunswick, Georgia, at the largest law enforcement training center in the world!! So, it would be wait and see for a while!

When I started teaching at Sabal Palm Elementary School in Tallahassee, I really enjoyed it! It was a little strange for our twin girls at first, because the guidance counselor and all the third-grade teachers thought the girls should be separated and put in different classrooms for third grade. I agreed, with some misgivings, but it worked out well! Both girls had more friends, and some different friends. Of course, there were times when Arien and Adrien still saw each other during the day: PE, music, art, lunch, etc., and of course they came to my room before and after school. I realized it was good for both of them. Although they continued to want to dress alike and wear their hair the same, Adrien and Arien did develop their own ideas and became more of their own person, not so much as half a set!

I was certified in many academic areas of special education: mentally disabled (educable and trainable), emotional behavioral disorders (EBD), and specific learning disabilities (SLD) in reading, written language, and math. One day, I was introduced to a new fourth grade student who would be in some of my classes. Danny was very pale, thin, and weak. After a couple of days, the school nurse set up a meeting in my classroom after school for fourth and fifth grade regular education teachers, as well as all special education teachers. The nurse gave all of us a first aid kit that had rubber gloves, masks, alcohol wipes, Band-Aids, etc., and taught us to treat everyone as if they were infected with AIDS, which was a big concern in those days. Even several nurses had been infected at Tallahassee Memorial Hospital when needles had pricked their fingers and brought blood even while wearing gloves. We were told if someone was bleeding, vomiting, etc., put your gloves on first, then and only then, give assistance! I suspected my new fourth grade student Danny was probably infected with AIDS.

The sweet little guy didn't return for fifth grade, and I couldn't get any information about him. He was well mannered, quiet, missed school more than most kids, and went to the school nurse for several medications throughout the day. There were many other children who also took medications from our nurse.

One afternoon as my girls and I were walking to our car after school, an older lady who was the school librarian, or the media specialist these days, stopped me. She got out of her classic cocoa brown Jaguar. She told me she heard on the car radio that Lucille Ball had just passed away! As we were talking and reminiscing about how funny Lucy could be, my girls got on the monkey bars. Adrien is the left-handed twin and Arien is right-handed. Adrien jumped off the monkey bars and was trying to be calm and quiet as she was holding her left arm close to her body. I realized that her left arm was badly sprained or broken! So, I had to end our conversation about Lucille Ball and told the sweet media specialist that I had to take Adrien to the emergency room at the hospital. Of course I called my husband, who was in Apalachicola, Florida, about 100 miles away, and told him what had happened.

Yes, Adrien's left arm was broken, and I think she may still have the cast from third grade! Adrien was also the daughter who got the end of her finger cut off on her left hand in the door slamming incident at our previous school, Shadeville Elementary.

Another fun day I had was when Arien's and Adrien's classes were both out on the playground at the same time on a Friday afternoon, with their respective fourth grade classes.

First, I had a student from Arien's classroom bang on my door and hand me a note from the school nurse. Arien had been hit in the nose with a soccer ball, and her nose was pouring blood— yes, it did look bloody and awful! Arien didn't cry…until she saw me.

Our nurse said that her nose did not appear to be broken, thank goodness, so I calmed Arien and myself and returned to my classroom. I had asked our nurse to let me know if the bleeding didn't stop and I would take her to the hospital. About ten minutes later I heard another knock on my classroom door, thinking that Arien's nose was still bleeding I ran back to the nurse's office. My other twin daughter, Adrien, had stepped in a shallow hole while running and playing kickball with her class, and her knee dislocated. When the P.E. coach picked Adrien up; her knee went back into place. She also was now in the nurse's office! Never a dull moment with my children especially on a "freaky Friday!"

After school was over for the day, I took Adrien and Arien to our pediatrician, Dr. James Penrod. He told us some girls seemed to develop this issue, especially with their hips and/or knees, but usually seemed to grow out of it.

Imagine how relieved I was! We had picked Dr. Penrod to be our pediatrician before the girls were born because he had an identical twin brother! His his brother was not a pediatrician, but he was a medical research doctor.

Dr. James Penrod also lived in our new neighborhood (Killearn Lakes) and had for several years before we moved there. When he met our son, Jason, who was fourteen years old, Dr. Penrod asked if he would babysit for him and his wife so that they could go out for the evening. Jason became Penrod's babysitter until we moved again! Jason could just ride his bike about half a mile to their home.

A funny story about our girls, was when I had taken them in for their three years old checkup. Dr. Penrod asked them if they knew their ABCs. They both said, "Yes," at the same time! However, I didn't realize they could take turns with every other letter: Adrien would say, "A." Then, Arien would say, "B." Then they just kept taking turns until they were finished! Dr. Penrod was shocked, and so was I!

At Sabal Palm Elementary School, a few days later, I was talking with one of the special needs teachers, Wendy, and she asked me about my family. She was especially interested when I told her about my brother, Louis Wayne Novak, and his wife, Sandy Novak, who were missionaries with New Tribes Missions. Wendy's brother and sister-in-law were as well! What a coincidence!

She was really concerned about her brother and other male missionaries in his group, who were taken away at gunpoint by the FARC in Columbia, South America. About 21,000 people had been kidnapped over the years and taken hostage by the FARC, which stands for "The Forces Armed for Revolution of Columbia."

My brother and sister-in-law had also received a copy of the tape from one of the wives of the kidnapped men. I assume all the missionaries in New Tribes Missions did it to show how dangerous situations can develop. We had listened to the tapes when my brother and his wife came to visit for Christmas. It happened to be the tapes with Wendy's sister-in-law and the other women in the group talking about what happened. It was hard to listen. They knew that their husbands were probably gone forever. The women and children had been saved and could let others know what was happening to the wonderful people who were trying to help those that needed help!

Another sad story: there was a cute little second grade girl in regular classes who walked a short distance to and from school every day with her fourth-grade brother. One morning, a car stopped, and the little girl was abducted by two men early in the morning! Her brother ran on to school and reported what had happened.

The police were called by office staff, and she was later found nude but alive, in a ditch close to our school! I didn't really know her, but I had seen her walk with her brother to school several times. I felt so sad for her family because she had been sexually molested!

In those days, there was a Very Special Arts Festival every year, which was based at the Leon County Convention Center in Tallahassee. I had even taken my students to the festival a couple of times while I was still teaching at Shadeville Elementary in Wakulla County.

A school bus always took us there with some of my students' parents who volunteered to take a small group around at the festival. It was a long drive there and back, but a lot of fun!

Florida State University always sent education students to help the teachers with their students. Parents were also invited to attend and take small groups around to watch and participate in helping the students make some of their own "art." There were bands from most of the middle and high schools, clowns with free helium balloons, and plenty of face painting opportunities. There were professional weavers, demonstrations of knitting, quilting, soap making, carding wool and turning it into yarn and knitting, making pottery, oil painting, and much more.

Joey's dad was the only man that came to my class at Sabal Palm Elementary, along with a few female parents, to ride the bus that took our special needs children to the Tallahassee Convention Center. I also had at least six cute young women students from the College of Education at FSU show up. So, I gave them each one to two students who would probably not cause any trouble. My paraprofessional and I took the most excitable children! Everyone had a great time, especially Joey's father; he couldn't take his eyes off all of the cute college girls all over the convention center! He kept trying to joke and flirt with them. He kept leering at all the young women and yes, he was married; His wife had to work that day. It really was embarrassing to most people in our group!

Later in the school year, we had another Florida State College of Education student come to observe and help my students. Her mother was the assistant superintendent of schools for the state of Florida! No pressure there!

As Joey bent over to pick up a book that he had dropped, my paraprofessional saw down the front of his loose shirt. She whispered to me that it looked like he had a pattern or drawing on his chest.

So, we called him into my office and asked what had happened to his chest. Joey admitted that his daddy (the only guy who went with us to the Very Special Arts Festival) got mad at little Joey. Then his dad put his size eleven sport shoe covered foot on Joey's little bird cage-like chest to make him be still! However, it was amazing that his father didn't actually break some thin little ribs!

I called our school nurse, and she came to my office. The nurse looked at Joey's chest and asked if his daddy was wearing shoes at the time. Joey said, "Yes!"

We could clearly see a pattern of some type of sport shoe bruised on his chest. She informed us she was required to take some photos of Joey's chest for documentation!

The school social worker assigned to our school contacted and interviewed us. I am not exactly sure what happened after that. The school year was almost over, and soon it would be summer. I do know that the social worker met with other people in their neighborhood and discussed the incident. The social worker in charge had weekly meetings with Joey, his mom, and dad throughout the summer.

When the three-member family was finally released from the weekly meetings, I never heard another word about Joey or his parents.

I just hope for Joey's sake that his dad learned a lesson about better parenting and followed through for his son's sake. Also, when sweet little Joey grew up, I hope he remembered how being physically injured by his father felt and how devastating it was to his spirit.

One day I had an individual education plan (IEP) meeting with one of my parents. If a child is placed in a special education program, an individual education plan (IEP) must be written and reviewed at least once a year.

At least three adults must attend the meeting: a classroom teacher that has the student in their class for part of the day, a parent or official guardian, and the special needs teacher that also works with the student is required to attend.

This student's mother was very sweet and complimentary to me and his homeroom teacher. She was very happy with her son's progress and success in school.

His fourth-grade teacher happened to ask his mother about her son's unusual first name. (Mom laughed as she thought about it.) The fourth-grade teacher asked if it was where he was born. Or where they had lived Mom laughed again and decided to tell us that she and her husband decided to name their son after the car that he was conceived in—a really small older Aston Martin!

I must admit, that was a first for me and the other meeting members! After she signed the paperwork from the meeting and left, the other people the room, could barely keep from laughing out loud!

Unbelievably, I had another parent that told me she and her future husband named their first child after a car that her future husband drove since they became pregnant in his Ford Edsel!

She was really a sweet woman and gave me presents throughout the two years I taught her son! I still have a beautiful, beaded powder compact that a woman can buy refills for. I always think of her son and his mother when I use it.

Richard was the number one shooter in his class out of sixty students and excelled in physical fitness at the Federal Law Enforcement Center when in Brunswick, Georgia.

Finally, the day came when I drove with all three children to Brunswick, Georgia from Tallahassee, Florida, to see Richard graduate from the largest federal police training center in the world, which was called The Federal Law Enforcement Training Center (FLETC) in Brunswick, Georgia.

Richard's parents even drove north from Lakeland, Florida, to see their son graduate.

Since we were staying in a nice hotel together, the grandparents took our three kids to dinner and then came back to watch movies on the television in the grandparents' room. This gave us some alone time, and we went out to dinner. Then we went to meet some guys who would be graduating with Richard and would also be newly minted federal agents tomorrow morning. Everyone was in high spirits, happy to complete a rigorous training program!

The graduation ceremony was very impressive. All the men were wearing suits and were very solemn at the time. Of course, there were speakers and awards handed out for various accomplishments during the training. My mother-in-law and father-in-law, our three children, and I were all suitably impressed!

It was an exciting time in all our lives because Richard, my husband, had finally reached his long-held goal of becoming a United States Federal Agent! First, we would be going on a paid house hunting trip to Key West, the total opposite of Alaska. We had to report to Key West, FL.in the coming spring. Maybe we would still one day get to live and work in Alaska. Our three children stayed with MeMa and Granddad Novak in Tampa, Florida, and so would Buster, our Boston terrier! Our other pets would be taken care of by one of Jason's friends who lived in our neighborhood in Tallahassee.

We decided that the kids and I would continue to live in our Tallahassee house until the end of the second school year. Richard worked in St. Petersburg, Florida, for several months. The kids and I continued to live and go to school in Tallahassee until a decision on a residence in the Keys was determined.

After careful consideration and looking at numerous houses, we finally decided that we would have a new house built on Cudjoe Key, at the twenty-two-mile marker from Key West. The house we selected was under construction. It was located on a saltwater canal and included cement dock for the boat. We would have a nice room under the house for storage of tools, large toys, small boats and oars, bikes, work benches, etc. Also, underneath the house would be a thick concrete floor to park our vehicles on, out of the weather.

There would be a sixteen-foot-high covered walkway all the way around the house to a screened back porch, which looked out over the canal. The porch provided a nice view of the canal and bay with tropical vegetation in all directions. The small yard had no grass but instead pea rock was used. We planted palm trees and gumbo-limbo trees along with fern.

Fresh, clean water is at a premium because the freshwater that people drink, cook with, bathe with and wash clothes with is piped in from the big lake in the lower part of the state of Florida, Lake Okeechobee! So, while our house was still under construction, we sold the lawn tractor and my two-year-old washer and dryer. Not to worry, our new house on stilts would be complete with a brand-new large stack washer and dryer in a closet with room for supplies and dirty clothes!

In the Keys a small thing that I noticed; restaurants don't serve a glass of ice water, only if you ask. It's a way of saving water and money!

Our family moved as soon as school was out, to the Cudjoe Keys. It was hard to leave our life in Tallahassee. But the adventure must continue.

We lived in a rental house that our builder knew about while our new home was still under construction. We were there for several months.

Even though we all were excited about the changes in our "latitude and attitude," it had been a hard trip! First, we had to rent the biggest U-Haul truck they had and pack all our furniture, decorations, clothes, dishes/pots and pans, potted plants, books, rugs and linens, outdoor furniture, etc. Jason rode with his dad in the front of the rental truck and took care of his guinea pig in his cage. We took our two cats (Amos was six months younger than our son, Jason) and Pepper, a two-year-old gray and white male cat. The cats were in the back of the truck with a litter box, plenty of dry food, and water. The girls rode in my new Cutlass Sierra that Pete, the peacock, loved. No, Pete didn't come with us. However, Buster, our Boston terrier was in the front in his bed on the floor. Chris, Jason's parakeet, was riding with us in the backseat with his cage strapped in. Also, Richard's maternal grandmother had recently passed away, and my mother-in-law wanted me to have some beautiful African violets that her mother had in her room for several years in the mountains of Virginia.

Finally, after a long, hard ten hours of driving, we pulled off the highway at a nice hotel, and the kids got into their swimsuits and had a great time in the pool. We walked Buster, fed and watered him, and Jason brought in his parakeet, Chris, for the night and let him fly around the room some. The guinea pig was fed and happy. The kids were happy because they got to swim and burn some energy. We ordered pizzas, salads, and cheese sticks with sauce and drinks. Finally, Richard and I went out and sat by the pool and had a nice relaxing and calming down time with a nice adult beverage, while the kids took turns showering and getting ready for bed.

We talked over our plan of how to unload our things, furniture, and just the essential items that we would need on a day-to-day basis. We would be living upstairs for several months in a rental apartment, and we would just unpack the bare minimum that we needed to live. Since the house was basically two self-contained apartments with lots of old furniture in them, we put most of our furniture covered with sheets in the corners and stacked close to the walls. Soon, we found out a family of three had bought the house! They agreed to let us stay for the duration of three or four months until our new house was completed. We did have a large bedroom upstairs in our unit where we basically stored lots of boxes that we didn't unpack.

Our twin girls, who were full of fun and loved to dance, would sometimes forget in the early mornings that we now had people downstairs. They started tap dancing as they made their breakfasts and packed their lunches. The new owners' bedroom must have been directly under our kitchen, because if the girls started tap dancing, someone would bang on the ceiling with a broom handle! Then, our girls would remember! Whenever we saw the wife or husband, no one ever made mention of the girls dancing on the upstairs kitchen floor!

After we finally moved into our new home, they even asked us if our girls could babysit for them several times and always paid them well!

Afterword
Sabal Palm Elementary, Tallahassee, Florida

I had so many wonderful students in my classes at Sabal Palm Elementary School. I really enjoyed my time there, and so did our twin daughters! When the girls and I went to Sabal Palm Elementary School for preplanning, the third-grade teachers advised me to consider placing them in different teachers' classrooms. Our girls did not like the idea at all; however, I decided it was probably the best option for both girls. They needed to stand on their own two feet and not depend on the other twin to take notes for them, etc.

The teachers and parents seemed to appreciate what I tried to do to help their children become better readers and writers and sometimes work on the student math skills.

Most teachers were very accommodating to my tight schedule and very friendly.

I had a wonderful paraprofessional for both years, and she helped me and the children as much as she could. She also had a daughter my daughters' age, and they became friends.

I had a great principal. He let me be in charge of the special education department. When I went to him and ask for another paraprofessional for one of the special education teachers or even another SPED teacher, he would listen to me and ask if we were making enough money to pay for another teacher or paraprofessional. I would be ready with the answers to his questions and tell him each regular student would earn x amount of dollars; however, a part time SLD student would earn two and a half times more than a full-time SLD student would only earn one time more, etc. I was always trying to help the special education teachers and SPED students get what they needed in supplies, more teachers, or paraprofessionals. I showed how much we were making above what was being spent, and he hired a new half-time teacher when necessary. I really appreciated his trust in my skills as a manager and teacher.

Finally, I would like to say thank you for being asked for my input as a special needs Teacher (who also got a master's degree in reading development and written language skills in children). I have always had a real interest in beginning reading and written language skills. I had several professors that were instrumental in helping to intrigue me to delve into this important learning area deeper.

Two great instructors come to mind from Florida State University that made me really enjoy their insights. The first instructor was Dr. Piazza; she was a young woman and made learning about beginning reading and writing skills very intriguing to me. It became a game for me to figure out what the young prekindergarten and kindergarten children, were trying to communicate in written form. I loved it! Thank you!

Also, Dr. Hafner wrote another book when I was finishing my master's degree in reading and written language. I was honored to read his latest book and thought about what he was trying to impart to the reader. I remember in one of his classes he would correct teachers for incorrect speech. I was glad he did that. How could a teacher impart knowledge to their students if they, themselves could not correctly speak English?

I was later asked by Dr. Hafner to be his teaching assistant for the coming college semester, and I would have been thrilled to have this position. It was always my dream to become a college professor at Florida State University. However, it was not to be.

I assisted in writing a book on beginning reading and writing skills which was published by the Leon County School System in Tallahassee, Florida, in the late 1980s.

As we traveled, I lost track of Dr. Hafner and Dr. Piazza. I will be forever grateful for the knowledge and experience that I received from them. I am still very intrigued in how the brain makes the connection between spoken and written language. For some it is easy and fun, and for others it is agonizingly difficult.

Jason still lives in Washington state and has his fish from Lake Monkey Business displayed in his game/exercise room. Now our son says he feels a little guilty about catching the fish just to hang on the wall. The poor fish gave his life to make Jason happy!

After we moved to the Keys, Docters advised we take Adrien to an orthopedic specialist in Miami. (for her knee issue) Her new doctor was known for his work with some of the Miami Dolphin Football players. Richard usually could change his schedule as needed when he was in town, so he usually took her to Miami for the doctor.

Adrien kept up well with Arien and their friends. She also had weekly appointments with a physical therapist in Key West at the hospital, as well. Everyone there loved our girls! Adrien was a hard worker and pushed herself because she was determined to get over the situation with her knee!

Chapter 4
Foreword

Horace O'Bryant Middle School, Key West, Florida
Monroe County

In pre-Columbian times, Key West was inhabited by the Calusa people. The first European to visit was Juan Ponce de Leon in 1521. As most of Florida became Spanish territory, a fishing and salvage village with a small fort was established.

In 1815, the Spanish governor of Cuba in Havana deeded the island of Key West to Juan Pablo Salas, an officer of the Royal Spanish Navy stationed in Saint Augustine, Florida. After Florida was transferred to the United States in 1821, Juan Pablo Salas wanted to sell, and he sold Key West for only $2,000 in pesos to John Simonton. John had bought the island because his friend, John Whitehead, had told Simonton about the strategic location. The island was considered the "Gibraltar of the

West" due to its great location on the ninety miles wide and deep shipping lane, the Straits of Florida, between the Atlantic Ocean and the Gulf of Mexico.

On March 25, 1822, Lt. Commander Matthew C. Perry sailed the schooner, Shark, to Key West and planted the United States flag, claiming the Keys as U.S. property.

Key West is now a city in Monroe County, Florida. The island of Key West is about four miles times two miles in actual size. It is a well-known seaport destination for many passenger cruise ships. The small Key West International Airport provides airline services to and from Miami for connecting flights. A plus is that the flight is amazingly beautiful, flying over the islands and the gorgeous colors of the ocean water.

At its closest point to a foreign country, Key West is only ninety miles to Cuba by water or plane! Key West is closer to Havana, Cuba, than it is to Miami, Florida! Tourists love to take photos standing by the ninety-mile marker on the island.

By 1889, Key West was the largest and wealthiest city in Florida. However, Key West was relatively isolated until 1912 when it was connected to mainland Florida by the Overseas Railway. However, the Labor Day Hurricane of 1935 destroyed much of the railroad, dumped many train cars full of people, and killed hundreds of residents trying to get away from the terrible hurricane. The Florida East Coast Railway Company, owned by Henry Flagler, could not afford to rebuild another railroad.

So, the United States government then stepped in and rebuilt the rail route as an automobile highway, which was completed three years later. The portion of US Highway 1 through the Florida Keys is called the Overseas Highway and is a beautiful drive.

In 1978, the Mayor of Key West, Charles McCoy, water skied to Cuba! Mayor Mc Coy did this to demonstrate the necessity of a continuing military presence in Key West. He had made the trip in six hours and ten minutes on a slalom ski! After that, there was no more talk of moving the military out of Key West!

In 1982, the city of Key West briefly declared its "independence" as the Conch Republic in protest over a United States Border Patrol blockade. The blockade was set up on US Highway 1 where the northern end of the Overseas Highway leads to the mainland of Florida at Florida City. The blockade was in response to the Mariel Boatlift. No one could go into or out of the Florida Keys, which relied heavily on tourism to survive.

Many proud residents of Key West refer to themselves as "Conchs." However, you can call yourself a "Saltwater Conch" if you were born in Key West!

When we found out that we would be moving to the Florida Keys, we all were excited. I called my mother and dad in Tampa, Florida, and told them where we would be moving and when. Then I asked them if they could keep Jason and our twin girls, Adrien and Arien, and our Boston terrier, during spring break for a week while we went on a house hunting trip in the lower Florida Keys. My parents agreed to keep them and seemed happy about it!

Our family would learn about another new area and live there for years!

Richard, after all his hard work, was now a United States Federal Agent in charge of the Florida Keys and Everglades National Park!

I interviewed for a 6th grade teaching position on the island of Key West! It would be a full-time, specific learning disability teaching position for all academics. The position was at the only middle school on the island at that time (the school was named after a famous educator, Horace O'Bryant).

I interviewed and was hired! I had letters of recommendation from other principals in Florida, which probably helped. I started at the beginning of the new school year in the fall.

The middle school was known for the almost professional circus it put on yearly. Performers from a professional circus based in Florida would be available to train the students to perform for a real circus performance. No animals were involved.

Many middle school families would volunteer to give free room and board to one or more professional performers for the duration.

The professional acrobats would be at physical education classes, helping as the circus grew closer. They would teach the kids to ride unicycles, to swing on bars and walk on tight ropes, plus balance on huge balls while walking around the stage and always wearing safety harnesses.

It was amazing, and everyone said the kids always worked so hard to do a great job.

Moving to the Florida Keys

Many years before tighter regulations were introduced and put into place, the canals had been cut through solid limestone rock. So, the canals had clear water with an abundance of small sea life. It was great that we would be able to keep our boat in the canal behind our new house.

Since we didn't have a mailbox yet, I put an old wooden chair where the mailbox would eventually be down the street in front of our new house. Then, I wrote our new address on the waxed cardboard box and placed it in the chair. I also thought to put a good-sized rock in the box so it wouldn't blow away, and it worked! I started getting mail soon after and never had any problems! Thank goodness, it was a dry time of year. It was funny, I never really expected the mail carrier to leave our mail and pick up outgoing mail! At that time, it was my only choice. I bet the mail carrier laughed about my impromptu mailbox!

While Richard was out of state, the kids and I drove the twenty-two miles to Key West several times to pick up some groceries and buy some new school clothes. When Richard returned, we drove to Cutler Ridge Mall just a little north of Homestead, Florida for shopping.

By the time school started back, we were ready! Myself as a teacher at Horace O'Bryant Middle School, Jason as a 10th grade student at Key West High School, and Arien and Adrien as 5th grade students at Sugar Loaf Elementary and Middle School.

Horace O'Bryant Middle School was the only middle school on the island of Key West when we moved there.

At the time, there were two elementary schools, and a special education needs school, May Sands, and one high school, Key West High School. Our son, Jason, attended the high school. The high school had a large indoor swimming pool, complete with a competitive swim team. The mascot of Key West High was the Conchs! There is still a huge plaster conch shell in front of the school.

There would be opportunities to go to the College of the Florida Keys for at least the first two years after high school. Some programs at the college are now four-year programs where students can earn their bachelor's degrees.

The theater at the college is named after a famous playwright, Tennessee Williams Theatre. Tennessee Williams lived in Key West for more than thirty years.

His famous quote about the area is, "I work everywhere, but I work best here, in Key West." His home has been turned into a museum, and Key West still has Tennessee Williams Day, complete with a parade yearly. The college is located on Stock Island, FL.

We moved into our new home on Cudjoe Key.

Soon, after we got back to our Keys house, we got an offer on our home in Tallahassee!

Papers were signed and faxed. It was over; no more worries!!

It was hard to really let go of Tallahassee since I had graduated from Florida State. I taught school at Sabal Palm for several years, and our girls went to school with me every day. P Jason went to middle school in Tallahassee for several years. Also, we had friends in the next county over from when we lived in Wakulla County and friends in Tallahassee.

We loved our new home on Cudjoe Key! It was fun living up high with the treetops! We had to climb sixteen steps to get to the front door! It was quite a chore to get groceries up the steps for a family of five people and one cat and Boston Terrier! So, we decided to institute a relay method. Everyone would stand in their place on the steps and pass the bags along to the next family member and it was no big deal. It was safer for everyone instead of trying to walk up sixteen steps with a bag of groceries in your arms. We call this process, The Chain Gang.

Richard and I both parked our vehicles under the house on a thick concrete floor that was the width and length of our new house. We also had a walkway sixteen feet high that wrapped around the entire house and connected to the upstairs back screened-in porch. Sometimes our dog would run back and forth on the walkway and just watch other people and dogs walking down the street. The girls basically took over the back porch with several aquariums: one aquarium was home for their medium-sized land turtle, and two others were homes for several hermit crabs. In the summers and when school was out on the weekends, a group of the girl's friends would come over and go swimming in the canal right behind our house. Each of our girls had a blow-up rubber boat with paddles, and their friends had similar types of equipment. Whenever the girls were in the water, I would be sitting in my chair on the dock and reading a book so I could make sure that all the kids were safe. After lunch, the girls would dress up in some of my old dresses, wear some old hats and purses, and even some old high heels, plus old jewelry, and pretend that they were teachers.

We had a closed in room built under our house with a six-foot sliding glass door for Richard's tools, workbench, bikes, boat equipment, etc. No lawn mower was needed—you can't mow white gravel! The entire lot was covered with white pea rock gravel, except for a couple of flower beds. Fresh water is sparse, and all potable water comes from Lake Okeechobee! The freshwater lake is the 3rd largest freshwater lake within the United States.

Freshwater pipes from the lake are bolted to the undersides of all the bridges going the length to Key West!

Jason worked throughout the summer as a construction helper and made quite a bit of money to spend on nice and expensive rods, reels, and tackle. He then started working at a small grocery store close to where we lived, and he could just ride on the sidewalk to work. Later, Jason started saving his money for a good down payment on a car. So, he got a part-time job at Winn Dixie on Big Pine Key.

When visitors travel the one road that goes through Big Pine Key, they see unusual tunnels and signs about Key Deer that list the them as another species of deer. They live free on the island and are about the size of a Doberman Pincer. If you try to steal, hurt, or kill any of the protected Key Deer, you WILL go to PRISON! They are on the Endangered Species List.

One day for fun, I started feeding the fish in the canal behind our house. The beautiful saltwater fish became so conditioned that every time someone walked on the dock, they would think it was feeding time! Then the fish would come up to get food!

I had to stop feeding the dry cat food to the fish because our neighbor saw me, and he started dropping food in. Then he dropped his fishing line in, complete with bobber and hook! He was catching my pet fish to eat!

Another time, our same neighbor decided to take a ride in their boat with their three-year-old son, Jackson, and his wife Paula. We always tried to look out for her and little Jackson when we were home. After the sky was starting to turn dark, I began to be concerned for the neighbors. Finally, when it was almost 9:00 p.m., Richard decided to call the Florida Marine Patrol, which is a state agency and asked them to look for the small boat and missing family. The Marine Patrol officers finally found them—the boat dead in the water out of fuel! The officers pulled the boat and passengers all the way back into our canal because of Richard's request as a friend.

Our next-door neighbors always seemed to have a problem! Their three-year-old son was always running or riding his tricycle around the neighborhood with no parental supervision- even at night! There were lots of canals full of water, and most houses were built up high in case of hurricanes and flooding of the canals. Thankfully, a local policeman found Jackson on the other side of our neighborhood still with his trike around 10:00 p.m. There were some streetlights, but there were not a lot of lights on because it was a school night. It was amazing that little Jackson didn't fall into one of the canals and drown!

Since we lived almost at the twenty-mile marker on US Highway 1, anybody who stopped at the neighborhood entrance could have quickly grabbed him and taken off with him, never to be seen by his family and neighbors again!

Even when both parents were home, they couldn't keep up with their precious boys!

One day when we came home from buying groceries, we found Jackson covered in lipstick and other old makeup! He was standing on our screened porch, sixteen steps up from the ground with an old purse I had given our twins when they played dress up. Poor Jackson! He was only three years old! I took him back to his father who was working on something in his workshop under his house. I was not happy, but mainly I was afraid for Jackson. I told his dad that Jackson could have been killed if he had fallen down the steps! His dad got angry and yelled that we should have locked the porch door! Not getting through to him!!

A week later, our daughters' land turtle disappeared. Tommy Turtle was about the size of a cereal bowl and had a nice environment in his aquarium on the upstairs back porch! I went back over to the clueless guy's house again and asked Jackson where our turtle was. Jackson said he took it outside to play! Of course, Tommy Turtle was gone! We just hoped that Tommy Turtle did not get thrown in the canal behind our house or run over by a car!

A couple of months later, we heard an ambulance driving up to our neighbor's home. Richard and I walked over to talk to Paula, the mother of Jackson, and his new baby brother, Samuel. Jean told me that she had put their new baby, Samuel (three to four months) in the bathtub with the water running while she went to check on the cookies that were baking! However, Paula forgot the time and when she went back to check on him, poor little Samuel was lying face down in the bathtub with several inches of water and was nonresponsive! These people were not teenagers, or even in their early twenties. The parents were at least in their late thirties or early forties!

The paramedics started working on the sweet little baby and rushed him to the hospital in Key West.

Paula asked our daughters, who were eleven years old, to babysit Jackson, her oldest son who was now four years old. While I was in her home, I realized that there were many disasters just waiting to happen: electric cords within reach, electric wall plug-ins without covers, a ten-gallon aquarium sitting on a flimsy stand that could easily topple over with rambunctious children playing and pulling up. The baby brother was released from the hospital after about a week. I never actually saw Samuel outside again. We all hoped that he would recover from his ordeal.

There were many students at Horace O'Bryant Middle School that were just friendly, wonderful kids. Most of the time they had awesome parents who were in the military and had lived overseas several times. There were even parents, especially women from other countries who had married American servicemen. I even had one mother who was from a Scandinavian country and had beautifully accented English.

However, there could be another side of some of my students. Some seemed to relish making jokes about some of my less fortunate kids and called them "rafters" if they had come to Florida on a homemade raft or a small boat from Cuba.

Also, some Key West families had been drug runners in those days, and they made a lot of money, so they flashed it around! The drug runners on the old tramp freighters from Columbia would carry the bales of marijuana and set up a rendezvous point and contact the local fishermen.

Sometimes they would have to jettison the bales, so they didn't get caught. The square grouper (fifty to eighty pounds) wrapped in plastic would sometimes wash up onto the beaches in the Keys.

The Key West drug runners and their families flashed a lot of real gold jewelry and money around. Even one of my sixth-grade students wore real gold chains around his neck and his wrist. He also wore a very expensive watch and always had the latest sport shoes and nice clothes. Lunch was only $1.50; however, James' mother gave him $5.00 every day to load up on ice cream and buy fresh baked cookies and ice cream for his "friends." I always thought that the only reason his "buddies" hung around him was that he always had money. Even then, he was about twenty-five pounds overweight, overbearing, and domineering. Most of my other students were sweet and overall, good kids!

Many of my students' mothers could barely speak any English, though they had lived in Key West for years. Most of them were maids in hotels or homes or cleaned fish when they worked in restaurants because they had little education and minimal English skills.

If I had to call a parent, it was always their mother, and she would usually be very humble. The mothers usually said that they wanted their children to get a good education. Then apologized to me for having to call. Usually, my students' mothers would ask to speak to their child. Then I could hear her cry and beg her child to be good. I would usually feel bad; however, I had to be able to teach and my students had to be able to focus on their classes.

I remember one Monday when I happened to be in the middle school hallway, and I overheard a couple of teachers complaining because one of their students that they shared had forgotten to put a set of dry clothes and a towel in his locker for Monday! Only in the Florida Keys! The poor "live aboard" kids had to swim or wade from their boats where most lived without electricity because their parents couldn't afford boat dockage fees at one of the marinas. So, the families would anchor their boat in a place away from the tourist areas, usually in fairly shallow water three to five feet.

That meant the kids must put their shoes in a plastic bag or tie their shoestrings together and hang them around their neck when they swam or waded through the water. They would have to unchain their bikes from the mangroves to ride to school while soaked in salt water. After that, they went into the school bathrooms to wash and dry themselves just using a bathroom sink and soap in a dispenser. Next, put on fresh clothes and put the wet clothes in their lockers in a plastic bag for the school day.

Since there was no electricity or running water on most of the boats, that meant the family members would have to use a bucket for bathroom needs. The bucket was

dumped over the side of the boat, hoping that there was a good current to take the contents away.

That's why local law enforcement groups and politicians have tried to enforce stringent laws about the "live aboard" people. Of course, there were other people who lived and still live fulltime at nice and clean marinas in the Keys. The marinas have electricity, fresh water, and plumbing. Some boats even have their own washer and dryers. Or, if not, the marinas usually have a coin laundry.

We had several teachers at Horace O'Bryant Middle School that lived on boats at marinas full time, and they also had washers and dryers on board. Some teachers had worked and traveled while living on their boat.

About a third of the teachers and paraprofessionals drove a scooter to school and didn't own a car since the island of Key West is only two miles by four miles in area.

It was the first time I had ever worked with male teachers that wore Bermuda shorts to school with untucked flowered shirts and sandals, and to top the look off, ponytails! In the Keys, in those days most women still wore dresses or blouses with skirts and sandals but not pantyhose. (It was just too hot!)

Some families lived on their big sailboats and would home school for a few years as their travels took them to many foreign ports. Then, as the children got older, they would enroll them in traditional schools. Most of the parents would invest in standard curriculums complete with books and other materials they would mail in when they got into a new port.

I also knew a few families with school aged children that owned homes in the Lower Keys where they lived for half the year during the fall and winter. Then they would travel back to their other homes in the northern states when the weather became more manageable.

I talked to a few teachers about it, and they said it worked okay. However, not seamlessly. If the children could adapt to having to study some subjects over and were motivated to be good students, the kids usually caught up and did well. However, sometimes the children had to be professionally tutored to keep up with the rest of the class. As a professional educator, I felt that it would be more difficult for many students as they navigated through the more intense higher grades. It would be difficult coming in and leaving friends again and favorite teachers before the end of the school year.

I remember a time in my classroom that really has stayed with me for all these years. I had a nice, respectful student from Cuba who had come over to Key West on a raft with his family. He was smart, cute, and very respectful. However, he did have a learning disability in reading, which would impact most subjects.

Ricardo was waiting by my portable classroom door early one morning.

He was grinning and excited! His poor, sweet mother had gotten him a new pair of white sport shoes for his birthday! He wanted me to be the first one to see them.

Of course, I bragged about how good looking the shoes were, and Ricardo was so happy! He had been wearing an old worn-out pair of shoes with string for laces since school had started. Now was Ricardo's time to shine and feel good about himself even if the shoes weren't really leather; they may have been his first pair of new shoes!

Then James, the meanest, most obnoxious student in my class, who was Caucasian and had more than anyone else in my classroom, came in, and Ricardo showed James his new shoes. James immediately jumped on one of his shoes and put a dirty scratch on it! James thought it was hilarious and made fun of Ricardo's fake leather sport shoes!

At lunchtime I called James' mother and told her about the shoe incident, and I asked her to help James write a nice and short apology note and have him bring it tomorrow. James' mother said he certainly would not write a note!

James was one of the heaviest kids in the whole sixth grade, and his doting mother usually gave him $5.00 a day for a lunch that would usually cost $1.50 in those days. So, he would have plenty of money to buy ice cream, popsicles, and fresh baked cookies from the cafeteria for himself and his friends.

James' parents had their own business complete with the latest equipment, such as fax machines, electric typewriters, and the latest computers and other equipment. James was the "baby of the family" and was spoiled and got anything he wanted!

I had a great paraprofessional at Horace O'Bryant with me most of the day. June rode her motor scooter to school every day with her son sitting on the back. June was always prepared for her reading groups and math groups. Sometimes, June tried to help a little too much; however, that was alright—at least

June worked hard and engaged with the kids and her job.

I had a 6th grade student who never seemed to stay on task during a lesson. He would start looking around the room, and I would have to call his name many times to engage him in the lesson. Then, I realized that he was asleep with his eyes still open! I would call his name, tap on his desk, snap my fingers, etc. Finally, I decided to call his mother in for a conference to discuss his inattention in class. He was missing most of his homework and classwork. He was failing most of his classes.

I felt that he could do much better if he could focus during his classes. I had spoken to his mom on the phone, but I wanted to make sure she understood how serious this situation really could be.

When I had called her before, I advised Robbie's mom to take the radio and television out of his room so he could concentrate and get more sleep at night. I told her that Robbie had a high IQ and should be performing much better. Robbie's mom told me that now, she would only let him have his television and/or radio on the weekends.

I had a suspicion that Robbie had developed a form of epilepsy, but I wanted a doctor to check him out before I said anything.

I was happy that Robbie's mother took my concerns seriously, and his mom took Robbie to his pediatrician. Robbie's pediatrician collaborated with another doctor, and they both confirmed what I already knew! Robbie had developed a milder form of epilepsy (absence seizure or petite mal seizure)!

Epilepsy has four basic types:
1. Absence/Petit Mal Seizures:
   a Causes a short period of "blanking out" or staring into space.
2. Atonic Seizures:
   a The seizure causes a person to have a sudden loss of muscle tone and go limp.
   b Can look like a head nod or drop, if severe, can cause a person to fall to the ground.
3. Atypical Absence Seizures
   a Blank staring, eye blinking, chewing movements, or lip smacking can include finger or hand rubbing
4. Clonic Seizures
   a Associated with repeated, rhythmic jerking movements lasting for a few seconds to a minute that cannot be stopped by restraining or repositioning

I believe I was the first teacher who had even suspected that Robbie may have a type of epilepsy. His mother said that no one had ever mentioned it to her as a possibility.

Robbie's mom was so happy that I was so concerned about her son. Robbie was prescribed different medications and was doing much better in all his classes by the end of the school year!

I was surprised when I started teaching at Horace Bryant Middle School that most kids would gulp their food and head out the back doors of the lunchroom!

I had to investigate where they went. It truly was amazing! There was a large, paved area behind the lunchroom, and most of the kids were trying to or waiting around to ride on various sizes of unicycles. All this was going on while in the background, great rock music was playing on large speakers!

Lunchtime had a fifteen-minute recess component built in! After lunch kids could walk around, play basketball, learn how to ride a unicycle, or play volleyball. Also, if you had a little extra money, you could buy an ice cream treat, a popsicle, or fresh baked cookies.

I was excited to be a part of the Horace Middle School Circus! Teachers always had some type of booth to make money for the school. Another special education teacher new to Horace O'Bryant wanted to work with me. We decided to fill large balloons with helium and tie them with ribbons to sell at the coming circus.

We sold almost every balloon and made several hundred dollars for our school! The food: hamburgers, fries, hotdogs, popcorn, cotton candy, candied apples, drinks, etc. were big money makers as well.

The school itself made thousands of dollars! The tickets to the circus made a lot of money. This money was used for materials, books, school furniture, and other supplies!

Horace O'Bryant Middle School was the first and only school where I kept a bag of popping corn for the chickens! Sometimes when my students came back to class, they would tell me that the chickens were back! They would be pecking in the grass outside my classroom door! So, I would give a student about a half cup of popping corn to scatter a little around for them!

Chickens are very popular in Key West. The Bahamians brought chickens with them when they originally came to the area. They would use them in rituals, and some still do. I assume they also ate some. Over the years, many chickens escaped captivity and now wander around the island of Key West. Sometimes I would see a dead chicken still with all its feathers, just missing a head and lying in the street!

Some people still practiced voodoo and rituals using chickens. When the last major hurricane hit the Lower Keys, many homes were devastated as were a lot of other buildings, trucks, cars, and boats. Many people in the Lower Keys, especially in Key West, tried to save as many chickens as possible that they could catch and put them into bags and pillowcases to move them to safety. They were somewhat successful, but many were still lost!

Our latest trip to the Florida Keys and Key West in particular, was three weeks in October 2023. Usually, you would see many little chicks, proud hens, and hear and spot colorful roosters all walking around in the open-air shops, bars, and restaurants. This time, we saw a few, but not a plethora of the famous fowl or poultry as in the past. Alas, people are no longer allowed to touch the famous feathered fowl or feed them!!

Fort Jefferson

Fort Jefferson's place in history is very interesting but is probably not as well-known as many other historical places during the Civil War.

The fort is located about sixty-eight miles from Key West in the Dry Tortugas, and there are only two ways to get there—by boat or by small floatplane.

Fort Jefferson served after the Civil War as the prison for Dr. Samuel A. Mudd. He was convicted of conspiracy for setting the broken leg of John Wilkes Booth, the assassin of President Abraham Lincoln.

Many of the doctors and nurses who worked at the prison became ill, and some died from yellow fever. Dr. Mudd volunteered to help the doctors and nurses that could work and helped save many lives-medical personnel as well as prisoners. For his work at the prison, his sentence was commuted to time served. Dr. Mudd was allowed to leave and live out the rest of his life a free man.

Now, Fort Jefferson is a National Park, located within the Florida Keys National Marine Sanctuary. People can buy tickets to go to the park by boat or seaplane. There are park interpretive rangers available to go on tours with you. The fort is in surprisingly good condition and is certainly a hidden gem from what you usually think of the keys. The boat ride that takes you there and back is very pleasant. Sometimes turtles and dolphins will swim along with the boats in the beautiful keys' water.

Sunset Celebration

In Mallory Square, where the cruise ships come in to dock in the afternoon, there is a huge party every day called "Sunset Celebration."

I especially liked the "Cat Man" in his tuxedo. He trained his cats to walk tight ropes and climb ladders, etc. One time he picked me to be his helper as a large crowd gathered, and since I love cats anyway, I really enjoyed myself! The "Cat Man" was French and told me that he had put his daughter through college with the money he had made over the years in Key West!

There were usually bartenders from local restaurants selling beer, wine, and mixed drinks from a loaded bar on wheels.

Another favorite guy is the "Tin Man." Many times, people can't decide if he is real or not. Of course, his clothes are silver, and his skin is covered in silver grease paint. When people come up to take photos of him, and with him, he will suddenly move and frighten them!

There is also a guy who does tricks on his unicycle, and it is very tall! He tries to help others who are brave enough to try more manageable unicycles.

There are all kinds of artists selling their wares: framed paintings, framed photos of the area, handmade jewelry, glass blowers, shell jewelry, carvings, and bright T-shirts.

In the background, there is always Cuban music pouring through the doors!

Of course, there are many restaurants and bars. Sometimes you may see a famous actor or singer in one of the local bars! Some famous actors and singers will even get up and belt out a familiar song!

Even now that we live in Georgia, my husband, Richard, and I still enjoy visiting the Florida Keys.

We used to travel by boat to Key West, but now we travel on our motorhome and pull one of our vehicles.

Since my husband is a Marine Combat veteran, we can stay on any military base throughout the country, and we have enjoyed many of them.

Chapter 5
Foreword

Sigsbee Elementary in Key West, FL and the Accident

Our twin daughters went to a beautiful school close to Cudjoe Key, where we lived. Sometimes they rode the school bus, and sometimes their dad or I could take them to Sugar Loaf Elementary/Middle School.

It was painted luscious strawberry pink and vanilla ice cream colors at the time. The school was elementary through middle school, K-8th grade. The girls were are twins and stood out academically.

One day when I picked Adrien and Arien up from school, the return trip home was thwarted by a bad accident on US Highway 1, close to our home. Since there is only one route up and down the keys, we couldn't return home for a while. So, we decided to do a little shopping in Key West and then have dinner at a favorite place. It turned out to be a four and a half hour wait on US Highway 1, mainly sitting in my car on a bridge.

Of course, wouldn't you know it? All three of us decided that we had to use the bathroom. Of course, there were no bathrooms on the bridge! So, I finally talked the girls into standing behind one of the open car doors and doing what they needed to do!

People were walking on US Highway 1 in the dark and complaining about missing their flights out of Miami.

Finally, we were able to cross the bridge and then were completely stopped again. Eventually, I could see the streetlight for the entrance road to Adrien's and Arien's school. Since no traffic was going to Key West because of the wreck, I decided to drive on the wrong side of the road and see if I could get far enough to make it back to Sugar Loaf Elementary-Middle School. I was hoping we could get to the school, use a phone, and get out of the car for a while.

It was not easy. I had to pull off the road because traffic was backing up since there was now another issue. A car trying to go to Key West had run out of gas and was stopped in the road where we were going to turn onto the street that would take us back to Sugar Loaf School. School buses were still at the school at 10:30 p.m. at night, and the bus drivers had unloaded the kids and were taking care of them in the cafeteria.

***

I had to go off road driving! My almost new Oldsmobile Cutlass was not made for off road travel!

We bounced, almost got stuck in the rocky soil, but finally made it past the car on the entrance road a quarter of a mile away.

At least we were back where there were bathrooms, coke and snack machines, and air conditioning! It was wonderful!

I had taken my school materials with me for the weekend to finish lesson plans for the next week. Since I had time, I got everything out of my car and completed planning for a couple of weeks for all my students and groups. At least I had turned lemons into lemonade! The lunchroom ladies were stuck too, and they started making ham sandwiches or peanut butter and jelly, fresh fruit or veggie sticks, juice, and milk to those who wanted it_all free! My girls had fun with their friends' playing games, etc. I was able to use one of the office phones and called my son, Jason, several times, but no answer all night long! So, I called the builder, who built our house, Mr. Jones, since Jason worked part time for him when he wasn't in school and weekends. However, the call wasn't very reassuring—he had not seen Jason all afternoon and there were no lights on in our house!

Mr. Jones said that he would call the Sugar Loaf School if he saw Jason on the island.

Mr. Jones did tell me that my husband, Richard, had called him and was very worried since he was at the Federal Law Enforcement Training Center in Georgia.

Mr. Jones said that Richard asked him to tell me that when I finally got home, no matter the time, please call him.

Finally, around 2:00 a.m., there was word that the road would be opening soon. Remember, lots of people had been stuck on US Highway 1 from 3:00 p.m. to 2:30–3:00 a.m., without food, water, and most without bathroom facilities!

Many were not actually sure what was going on since there were no cell phones at the time! If they had a working car radio, they could have found out some information. Several cars were stranded because they had run out of fuel. The girls and I finally made it home around 3:15 a.m. I called Richard and let him know we were fine but tired.

Then, Jason finally showed up! Who knows where and with whom a sixteen-year-old boy was with all day and night!? I wasn't in a mood to talk with him at that time of morning.

The kicker was that I had to get up at 6:00 a.m. on Saturday morning for a required workshop on another island, further up the Keys.

I was required, as all special education teachers were in Monroe County, to recertify yearly in certain areas. Safe takedown techniques for teachers was the training required….go figure!

After two and a half of sleep, I made it on time for the workshop and was recertified.

The worst thing was, with only two and a half hours of sleep, I couldn't drink coffee or hot tea because I'm allergic to caffeine!!

Sigsbee Elementary
Sigsbee Navy Base, Key West, Florida

The second year, I got a chance to move to Sigsbee Elementary School, which is located on Sigsbee Navy Base in Key West.

There is also another military base in the Key West area called, Boca Chica Naval Air Station. Every day before and after school, I usually saw the airplanes flying overhead as the pilots practiced flying those amazing planes! The sights and sounds of freedom!

Sigsbee was a great school, and I really enjoyed my time there! I taught a self-contained class from kindergarten through fifth grade! We were like a little family in my classroom. My principal thought that I was fabulous! He said he admired my ability to schedule classes and handle kindergarten through fifth grade students in the same room, sometimes at the same time.

I had a wonderful paraprofessional—she was top notch! My paraprofessional, Linda, and I worked well together and separately. It was imperative that we follow our schedules closely.

I got the "special classes" schedules such as art, music, computer, physical education and Spanish for each grade level with times listed. Then we had to stay on time! I set up the class like schools that use the Pod System. So, K–1st grade would be in a certain area, 2nd to 3rd in another space, and finally 4th to 5th grade.

We all went together at lunchtime. The older kids sat at the end of the tables, and the younger ones sat at the beginning of our tables.

I was impressed by the military police who stood on guard duty every day. Each car would have to stop at a closed gate and each person in the car would have to show their photo identification badge. If everything was in order, the electronic gates would open. If not, the car would be denied and would have to turn around and leave.

If we were at an "Under Threat Level," not only did we have to show our badges, but we also had to wait while the guards on duty swept under each car with mirrors on long poles. This was to make sure that there were no bombs attached underneath our cars! I thought it was interesting! During the conflict, "Desert Storm," people coming onto the base had to give themselves an extra twenty to thirty minutes every morning to be cleared before the gates would be raised to allow entry one car through at a time!

My principal ran a "tight ship." Every morning, all students at the school would line up on the outdoor basketball court with their class. Each teacher knew where their students' line-up spot was for the year. The first student would stand by their teacher's number, and from there would make a straight line. When the bell rang, there would be a "show of colors." A large United States flag would be carried on a long pole by the boy scouts or girl scouts. There was a microphone, and a fifth grader would lead the "Pledge of Allegiance." Next, there would be a "moment of silence." Then the students from each class would walk in a quiet line led by their teacher. Very orderly and amazingly quiet halls!

Parents always came to the parent/teacher conferences. If they didn't, they would be in trouble with their commanding officer!

Most of my students had traveled and lived in several states and countries. However, they didn't think much about it because it was the only life they had known.

At Sigsbee Elementary, there was always a Halloween parade every year. All the kids were in costumes, and so were the adults that worked at the school! I was a little surprised; however, we were in Key West! Everyone would come out of their offices and houses on base in uniform and line the streets to see their kids and teachers parade down the parade route. It was a fun day! Later in the afternoon, there would be classroom parties! Remember, in Key West, October Fest is celebrated every year and a big deal even now!

My students had some wonderful parents; however, there were a few wacky ones! Sometimes I would have a mother that could barely speak any English, and her husband would have to translate for me.

I had to call one of my student's mothers and tell her that the school nurse said her son had lice. The mother informed me that it wasn't lice but, just fleas from their dog! Was that any better? She said she would treat Matt's hair with flea and tick shampoo. I worried that it would make her son sick. She assured me that he would be fine; she had used it on him before!

Patrick's mom wrote a letter that indicated she loved to attend conventions for Star Wars fans and, she would be leaving on a bus trip in a few days. She also said that she would be gone for a week. She loved to dress up like Princess Leia and was taking a new costume and new wig!

Later that school year, when fifth grade graduation was approaching, a parent wrote a note and said Johnny didn't have dark dress shoes, and she confided that she didn't want to spend money for leather dress shoes that he would never wear again. It was a requirement to wear dark dress shoes. So, I came up with a plan. I urged her to buy some thick black liquid polish and go over his cheap, old white plastic sport shoes with a couple of coats of the polish. She did, and the shoes looked pretty good! Problem solved!

My principal at Sigsbee Elementary was part owner of an offshore boat racing team. He handled the throttle on the boat! My husband, Richard, and I really liked the boat races. They were always filmed from low flying helicopters with the photographers strapped in but partially hanging out of the doors to get good movie film and still photos.

When we lived in the Lower Keys, we always attended the Offshore Power Boat Racing Series every year! The boats of choice had Catamaran hulls or Mono hulls. They were loud, and they were fast! The course was marked with large, bright orange-colored floats anchored into place.

My husband, Richard, all three kids, and I loved the boat races! Just think, we were in our boat with many more boats, in the beautiful aqua blue water with boat racing fans! We were close enough to the race boats and could see the drivers and throttlemen in their beautiful and powerful boats! It was exciting for all, and of course, it was loud. Of course, the spectator boats were all behind barriers anchored underwater.

Sometimes the cameramen would fly over the spectator boats and film us! We would have lunch on our boat and have lots of cold drinks and water!

While we lived in the Lower Keys, there always seemed to be something going on! street fairs, contests, and sunset celebrations were popular!

One thing that you could count on every year in October was October Fest! There would always be a parade through the city of Key West. However, we found out the first time we went that it was not really a family type event! It was a pretty risqué event! Usually there would be many floats and lots of performers walking.

There were men dressed as women, and women dressed as men. Sometimes the beautiful costumes were just painted on the totally nude individuals! However, the body paint was very professionally done. From a distance, you would see guys dressed in snug tuxedos.

However, when they got closer, you would realize the "costume" was just beautifully painted on the nude, shaved bodies!!

Also, there were women who looked like they were wearing beautifully designed and embroidered leotards. Then you would be amazed that the entire costume was beautifully painted on their nude bodies!

Others would barely be dressed in very short skirts without underwear. The first time we went, we took our kids—never again!

There were many fun family times we had with all three of our children in the Florida Keys. We would take a picnic lunch and go from Cudjoe Island (at the twenty-mile marker) on our boat and go exploring on different small, uninhabited islands. We would go swimming in the aqua blue water or walking on the beach looking for hermit crabs and shells.

Many times, our kids and my husband, Richard, would swim with snorkels and masks. They would discover wonderful small coral reefs, lots of beautiful fish, and a plethora of other creatures.

Someone had to stay on the boat and watch for sharks, barracuda, and other creatures. Of course, it was always me! I was uncomfortable knowing what lurked in the water, and when five to six feet long barracudas would show up, snapping their teeth, while following Richard and the kids, I would bang on the side of the boat with a paddle. Then I would warn them that it was time to get out of the water for a while. Thank goodness, no one in our family was ever attacked! There were several attacks by barracudas while we lived in the keys and some shark attacks!

One lady was wearing a gold bracelet on her wrist, which caught the attention of a large barracuda, who probably thought it was a small fish, and took her right hand off.

I remember that she lived on the next island near us, and they had fund raisers for her to get a prosthetic hand.

Another day, a woman earned the attention of a hungry barracuda by wearing big gold earrings and it took her left ear.

To be fair to the barracudas, they probably thought the gold flashing in the water was a small fish.

We also had great times at American Shoal Light. The water is so clear around the lighthouse that you can see the metal legs of the lighthouse as they go down and down in the clear, deep and beautiful aqua water.

All three of our children and my husband would jump into the water and float around. Wearing a mask, they would look deep in the crystal-clear water and see many species of beautiful fish.

On a windy day, when the water would be very choppy, we would go on the backside of some of the islands and still be in calm water!

Since we lived on Cudjoe Key, we would sometimes go fishing by the Seven Mile Bridge, and then we would have a simple picnic lunch. We pulled up onto a small island with the kids and our Boston terrier so they could run around for a while.

An amazing place we really enjoyed was John Pennekamp State Park; it is now part of the Florida Keys National Marine Sanctuary. From our boat you could see many beautiful living coral reefs and a plethora of beautiful fish.

Many times, we took our boat down to Key West for the day, especially when we had friends or family who would come to visit us in the summers.

Sometimes, especially in the summers, we could see a large waterspout just starting to form and coming towards us! We would try to outrun it or go in another direction.

One time, a friend who lived just a few houses from us on the same canal was on the water in their boat when a storm suddenly came up, and, before he could get himself and his family out of 'harm's way, his boat was struck by lightning and the windshield exploded. However, thank goodness, no one was seriously injured.

The island of Key West itself, is not a very large island. It is around two miles times four miles and is only eighteen inches above sea level.

Key West has had many famous people visit and live there over the years. There is a story about one such individual that many say is true. It is about Ernest Hemingway, the famous author, bigger than life adventurer, sportsman, and journalist. Hemingway brought his new wife to Key West where they decided to buy a beautiful home.

According to the story, he left his new wife while he went traveling abroad for a new book. While he was gone, his wife had built a very nice in ground swimming pool and decorated their new home with her husband's money.

When Ernest Hemingway got back to Key West, he told his wife, "Well, you've spent my last penny!"

If you go to the Hemingway House, you can still see the penny that he had cemented on the deck around the pool!

Hemingway lived in Key West all through the 1930's. His home is now the Hemingway Museum. It is also the home of the descendants of the original six toed cats that Hemingway had. There are around 40 of the six toed cats on the property currently.

Key West has an Ernest Hemingway lookalike contest every year. Several famous designers, writers, and movie stars own houses or restaurants in the Lower Keys.

When we lived in the Florida Keys, we would sometimes go by Monkey Island, which is close to Cudjoe Key.

Sometimes when we passed the small island, we would see descendants of monkeys who years before were used in medical research. When that ended and the people were trying to put the monkeys in traveling cages, many ran off and even swam to other islands.

The monkeys that are still there are descendants of the monkeys that were used for pharmacological testing before laws were enacted to ban that practice. Some of the monkeys have thrived on their own, living on the mangrove covered islands.

Afterword in the Keys

The time we lived in the Florida Keys passed too quickly! After several years of living and loving the Keys, it was time to move again! This time we would be moving to Brunswick, Georgia, where I would teach middle school children at Risley Middle School. That was nice because our girls would also be at the same school. We would be able to ride together again!

Later, during the summer, one of the bad storms that typically blow through or go around the Keys hit the Miami Mall, where we used to do our school and Christmas shopping. The beautiful mall, surrounding shops, restaurants, and beautiful neighborhoods were destroyed!

There was also a lot of damage on many of the islands in the Florida Keys.

Some of our friends lost their homes and everything in them plus their vehicles!

We had only just moved to Brunswick, Georgia, at the time, and were still living in temporary quarters!

Most of the Florida Keys have a thriving seafood related industry with boat captains willing to take tourists or locals out (chartering) the boat for a few hours or a whole day if wanted.

Chapter 6
Foreword

Risley Middle School, Brunswick, Georgia

The oldest Native Americans in the surrounding area of Southeast Georgia are believed to be the Guale Indians. They mainly lived at the Altamaha River on Sapelo Island and probably on Saint Simons Island in the 1500's.

In 1569 missionary work was undertaken by the Jesuits who were among the Cusabo and Guale Indians. One of the missionaries, Domingo Augustin, wrote the grammar of the Guale language. However, the missionaries soon abandoned the country.

A few years later, in 1573, missionary work was resumed by the Franciscans and was more successful. In 1597 there was an upheaval when all the missionaries, but one, were killed.

Many Guale towns were then destroyed by the white men, which reduced most of the Indians to submission.

By 1601, the rebellion was basically over. Many native people who did not escape inland moved, or were moved in 1686, to small islands. Some Guale Indians appeared to have made it to South Carolina. In 1702, there was another uprising, and the remainder of the Guale Indians and small numbers of other tribes made it to South Carolina to live with the Creeks (later called the Seminoles).

The Guale were last heard from in 1719 in the Saint Augustine area. It is believed that the Guale Indians died out.

Fort King George on the Darien River in Georgia has more information on the Guale Indians recounted.

The Altamaha River Water Shed is the second largest on the east coast of the United States, with Chesapeake Bay being number one.

More water flows into the Atlantic Ocean from the Chesapeake and Altamaha Watershed than any other rivers!

The Beginning of Brunswick, Georgia

The first English settler in the area, now named Brunswick, was Mark Carr, a captain in General Oglethorpe's Army.

Brunswick, Georgia, dates to 1738 when Carr's plantation of 1,000 acres was established along the Turtle River.

Brunswick got its name from the ancestral home of King George II of Great Britain (Brunswick- Luneburg) in Germany.

In 1771, the royal province of Georgia bought Carr's fields and laid out the town of Brunswick in the grid style of the Oglethorpe Plan. Much of the Victorian architecture and signature squares still stand.

In 1789, Brunswick was named one of five original ports of entry for the American colonies. Shortly after, Brunswick was named the county seat of Glynn and still carries that distinction to the present.

During the Civil War, much of the city was destroyed including the four-story Oglethorpe House Hotel, which was actually built in 1835 and was burned down in 1862, never to be rebuilt.

During the 19th century, businesses were again thriving due to a large lumber mill, good port business for cotton, seafood—especially oysters—and tourism due to nearby Jekyll Island, where millionaire's row of beautiful homes, hotels, and restaurants still exist.

World War I stimulated ship building in Brunswick. When 16,000 workers were employed: black and white, men and women, to produce ninety-nine Liberty Ships and "Knot" ships during World War II, the economy boomed!

Brunswick's Glynco Naval Air Station was for a time the largest blimp base in the world! The Naval Air Station was built in 1942. Two blimp hangars were built at Glynco. They were 1,058 feet long, 297 feet wide and 182 feet high.

Each hanger housed 8 blimps. Concrete pylons at each end were connected by massive wooden trusses and a shingled roof.

In 1949 Glynco became a Naval Air Training Facility and added an 8,000-foot runway.

Glynco trained naval jet pilots and air traffic controllers until 1974, when the base was decommissioned.

In 1975 the Glynco Facility was once again put into use by the Federal Government when it became the Federal Law Enforcement Training Center and remains as such at this time.

Of course, over the years the Federal Law Enforcement Training Center has upgraded, added more programs, and now trains 103 different federal agencies.

The economy of Glynn County owes a huge amount of gratitude to the Federal Government for locating the training center in Brunswick, Georgia. Many businesses and neighborhoods have seen great growth due mainly to the training center.

Also, the Glynn County School System has benefited from the parents with federal jobs and their children who attend Glynn County Schools due to the "Federal Impact Money" for each student.

Brunswick continues to have a thriving economic activity centered around its deep natural port, which is the western-most harbor on the eastern seaboard.

There is another port in Glynn County, Colonel's Island Terminal Roll On, Roll Off, which is owned and operated by the Georgia Ports Authority. It is the second largest RoRo port in the United States and has the largest auto-handling facilities, as well as one of the most environmentally conscious ports.

Glynn County has been noticed by professional movie companies, and parts of many films have been shot in Glynn County at the beaches and especially on Jekyll Island including the port in Brunswick and even in downtown, using the old buildings that are in good repair.

The Old Town residential and commercial district is the largest small town on the urban National Register of Historic Places in Georgia!

Many old stores, banks, etc. have been repurposed and turned into offices, restaurants, breweries, apartments, and an upscale new hotel with an open-air restaurant on the top floor!

Glynn Academy was the first public building built in 1819, but it was founded on February 1, 1788, making it the second oldest high school in Georgia. For more than one hundred years, "Glynn Academy" included all grades from first grade to senior high school. The "Old Glynn Academy Building," now known as "Alumni Hall," was built in 1840.

It is the oldest wooden schoolhouse in Georgia. For more than fifty years, this building served as the only public-school building in Brunswick.

The city of Brunswick was officially incorporated as a city on February 22, 1856. In 1860 the city had a population of 468 people.

In 1878, poet and native Georgian Sidney Lanier wrote his world-famous poem, "The Marshes of Glynn," based on the salt marshes in Glynn County as he sought relief from tuberculosis in Brunswick's milder climate.

Currently, in Glynn County, the area is consistently updating or building beautiful new schools, updating old parks, and even building beautiful new parks. Plus, repurposing old buildings apartments and offices.

From the Florida Keys, to Brunswick, Georgia

My husband, Richard, would be detailed to the Federal Law Enforcement Training Center (FLETC) in Brunswick, Georgia, after his duty station in the Florida Keys ended that summer. Such is life with the federal government—always on the move.

We sold our two-year-old house on Cudjoe Key for a nice profit and would close the day before we moved.

On Spring Break, we decided to go to Brunswick, Georgia, on a house hunting trip, and I had already set up an interview with the principal at Risley Middle School. I also had a phone interview with the special education Director for Glynn County Schools. I had my interview with the principal of Risley and was hired!

We also met with a realtor on our trip but were unable to find a home we really needed and wanted in such a limited time.

Our realtor promised that she would continue to look and would have more properties to show us when we actually moved to Brunswick in a couple of months.

When we arrived at Brunswick, we were going to be living in "temporary accommodations" at a Brunswick hotel. Our furniture and most of our belongings were put in air-conditioned storage in Savannah.

We had two connecting hotel rooms with a complete kitchen and a nice storage room, and two bathrooms. Since we would buy new school clothes in Brunswick and maybe Savannah. I packed my sewing machine, iron, ironing board, scissors, and thread. Our twins were hard to fit since they were small for their age.

I celebrated my birthday at the hotel out by the pool, and then one month later, the girls celebrated their birthday.

I won't say it was easy living in two hotel rooms with a total of two adults with an almost seventeen-year-old teenage boy, twin twelve-year-old girls and three pets because it wasn't.

Sometimes I would cook or order in, but most of the time dinner time would find us at a local restaurant. We were lucky because the federal government paid our packing and moving expenses including temporary quarters and Per Diem

We began our search for a home. We looked at established homes and property in nice family areas, not too far from the schools. We were hoping for more space for the kids in a safe neighborhood. We went back and forth about building or buying a home.

When we first saw our house in an established neighborhood, I liked the floor plan, the large backyard, the beautiful inground pool, and the placement of the house on a nice lake.

We when we returned from a visit to my parents' house in Tampa, and after looking at many other homes, I was ready to buy a house that was ready to go. Other people must have complained about the dark butterscotch color of the big two-story house and the dark chocolate trim because the house was still on the market. When we returned to the house, it was now a pale yellow with white trim and white shutters!

We made an offer on the house, which the owners finally accepted.

Finally, the day came for the closing on the house and property, and then it was ours! After living in a hotel for almost four months, we were ready to have our own furniture, dishes, sheets, etc. We were ready for a real home again!

We moved in right before Halloween. It took a lot of work from all of us! The moving van arrived from Savannah, and I had met them at our new home.

The kids were in school; however, I had to take the day off on a Friday to let the movers in and direct where the boxes and furniture would go.

I told my students that if I got a good report from the substitute teacher, on Monday, I would have a good surprise for them! Of course, it would be food; teenage boys are usually all about food.

I tried to direct the furniture and boxes coming in and show the moving guys where to put the boxes and furniture. Up and down the stairs the guys trudged. They were busy putting four beds together and table legs on tabletops.

Our one-year-old Boston terrier, Beau, and our elderly black cat, Amos, were disturbed to say the least. I knew I had to get things in some semblance of order. Chris, Jason's parakeet, was flapping his wings a lot. The weekend would be over quickly, and Monday, back at school, was looming for all of us.

Then, the wallpaper ladies showed up—pulling off and putting up new.

The former owner of our new home was happy to meet us to show us how to run the inground swimming pool equipment.

When we had moved during July and I went back to visit my new school, where I would teach students with specific learning disabilities, I was surprised!

I discovered that my new teaching position had been changed without my knowledge! My teaching position was changed from specific learning disabilities (SLD) to emotional behavioral disorders (EBD)! These are usually the most difficult kids to deal with! The EBD students are all boys and are usually mad at the world because of all the trauma they have experienced in their lives!

I was surprised to say the least! Then I found out that I would have to take a half day test at a testing center in Savannah, Georgia, eighty miles north of Brunswick.

I knew I could pass the teachers' exam, but I would need to brush up on criteria to qualify a student for the Emotional Behavioral Disorders designation, and the teacher must know the criteria well to pass.

After teaching special needs students for fifteen years, I was able to pass the exam with great scores. Directions I was now certified to teach another area of "special education" or "exceptional education", a three area certifications!

Within that time frame, I had to take a couple of classes, and when I passed them, I would be certified for five more years.

As I taught at the old Risley Middle School, I began to realize that the last school year had been terrible for the students with emotional/behavioral disorders, or E/BD, and their teachers! Yes, teachers!

In one school year, there had been two different female teachers in my position and one male teacher! None had lasted more than three months!

I knew the students weren't going to make me leave, because even though I was smaller than most of my students, I don't give up easily, and I can be very stubborn!

As I was looking through my individual educational plans, or IEPs, on my caseload, I realized there had been terrible problems for the kids and the teachers! An IEP is what it sounds like—a school/learning plan for each individual special needs student.

It can be very detailed with how to best present and teach that one student. It will have educational goals, behavioral goals, and how materials should be presented and how to evaluate the student's mastery of the goals that are presented. The IEP for that individual student needs to be updated (at least once a year). More often if the student is doing well and mastering the goals listed on their IEP or if the student is having serious difficulties it is updated. If or when the IEP is updated, the parents, at least one, or a legal guardian, must attend as well as one of the student's regular classroom teachers, and the special education teacher must be present to lead the meeting.

Hours in the special needs class may be increased or decreased. The student may even be taken out of special needs classes altogether if the committee feels that it is warranted. These changes are due to great improvement or failure to improve and cooperate with adults and/or students. The student may refuse to cooperate with anyone and may be termed socially maladjusted and a regular education setting may not be the right place for such a student. They may not improve in the regular school setting; they may need to constantly earn points to get to participate in most activities or lose points if they don't. Usually, it is called alternative school. In all my thirty-five years of teaching, I only sent two of my students to an alternative school setting!

All hours in the special needs classes may be dropped altogether if the regular education classes are more appropriate for the student at the time. A special education meeting must be held to determine that. A parent or legal guardian must be in attendance and sign the forms.

The exact opposite may also take place—the student is not meeting their goals and is not progressing academically and/or emotionally. So, hours may be increased if needed at a meeting where a parent or legal guardian must attend and sign the forms.

None of the three teachers, in one year, had stayed longer than three months or left any directions before throwing in the towel; not one teacher left any directions or reasons for their hasty departures! Now I know what they had gone through! Some of the most severely disturbed emotional behavioral disordered (EBD) kids who didn't trust anyone and hated everybody!

On Fridays, some of my 8th grade students were taken on a school bus and monitored by a special education teacher as they got the chance to learn work skills.

Some of the students worked at Walmart, different plant nurseries, Home Depot, and Lowes, usually in the plant nursery areas or sweeping floors, taking out trash and putting merchandise on the shelves, and so on.

A couple of my students were unable to handle the freedom and stole gold chains from the jewelry cases in Walmart! They called it "five finger discount." It was called stealing by the managers, and my students lost their Friday jobs and were suspended from school!

I had some kids whose mothers would just walk around the neighborhoods, trying to sell beef roasts or steaks they bought with food stamps. They were trying to get enough money for illegal drugs they craved!

The kids in my class would taunt the boy whose mom was seen trying to sell wrap

meat so she could buy her illegal drugs. Then there would be a fight, and I would have to call the office for help! I did not try to break up a fight between two teenage boys; they were too tough and strong. Our young male teachers always came to help. Our male principal was always there when I needed his help. The students were in detention for the rest of the day. They were not allowed back in the classroom until a parent or guardian met with me and the required school staff. The meeting was held to determine the appropriate action for the student.

Some of my kids had to wear ankle bracelets ordered by the local judge for petty crimes. the. They had to wait until the general school population was inside the buildings before, they were escorted to my classroom.

Those students were only allowed in my classroom. Breakfast and lunch were sent to them every day in my classroom. In the afternoon, the reverse happened. Those boys were escorted out of my room early, before the bell rang, and were loaded back on the bus. In addition, those students were not allowed outside all day. They were taken home and required to remain there. On the weekends they were required to work at the parks, clean up trash, sidewalks, etc. If they were not at their jobs and their homes when they were supposed to be, they would be driven immediately to the juvenile detention facility to serve the remainder of their sentence. That went on for about six months.

Some of my students had horrible situations play out in front of them as they watched. I really felt terrible for them! No children should ever have to see such horror and misery in their own families!

Dear Mrs. Smith

I had one teenager in my class who saw his dad shoot his mother to death at the kitchen table because he didn't like what they were having for dinner! A mother of one of our former students discovered her former boyfriend was living with a new woman. So, she barricaded the windows and doors late at night using duct tape and sealed the windows and doors with duct tape, splashed gasoline over the trailer and threw a couple of matches. I believe that both people in the trailer died.

The school zone for the old Risley was mainly in a poor area, and many of the parents were poorly educated, but they wanted better for their children, and I respected that.

One of my student's parents was a police officer, and he was tough on his son, Phillip, who was a part-time student in my class.

After school, Mr. Marks, my principal, brought Phillip and the other boy who started a fight, to my room, and in a few minutes, Phillip's dad, the policeman, showed up.

Both boys' faces were red, and they could barely see out of their red, bloodshot eyes because of some type of strong red pepper flakes that the other boy had brought from home.

It seemed that Phillip had been having problems with the other kid, who was taunting and making fun of him because he was in a special education class.

Right after school when the buses were loading, the other kid reached in his pocket into a plastic bag and threw red hot pepper pieces and seeds into Phillip's eyes, and he literally couldn't see! However, Phillip got in some punches and threw hot pepper pieces back into the face of the other guy.

Phillip's dad, the policeman, was angry at his son for not beating the instigator to a pulp! I tried to intercede on Phillip's behalf, but Phillip was in shock and really didn't know who or what had hit him in the face and his eyes. That really didn't connect with Phillip's father!

My students were all emotional behavioral disordered (EBD) kids and were mostly tough boys with hard lives and mad at the world! Most lived in the projects or terrible, old, and nasty trailer parks in trailers that their parents rented. Some lived with grandparents or other family members. There was usually no father figure in the home. With all that extra baggage, it made them especially hard to get to emotionally and mentally. Of course, they were suspicious of another white teacher who would probably quit after a few months!

One day, a favorite student, Ronnie, told me, "Look, Mrs. Smith; you just can't understand us. You're a "preppie!" I thanked him in front of the class. Then, everyone laughed! (Which is what I wanted and expected.) I asked him what he thought prep or preppie really was. He laughed, and so did most of my class. However, he couldn't or wouldn't put it into words. So, I explained to the class that being called a "preppy or prep" can be a compliment! It can mean that you are dressed neatly, clean, well groomed, and are trying hard in school for your life's work later. You are [preparing] for your future life and work later when you grow up! You don't have to be rich, but you need to work hard at whatever you do. This sort of calmed the kids down! It gave most of the older boys something to think about.

Ronnie was a great baseball player, was a good student in his regular education classes, and in my classes as well. Sometimes he seemed mad at the world. Ronnie had enjoyed a pretty good life until his father died on his shrimp boat of a massive heart attack at the age of forty.

Ronnie's mom had not needed to work full time before her husband had died. Now, Ronnie and his family were barely scraping by, living in an undesirable rental trailer in an old rundown trailer park. His mom was working a lot of hours just to get by. Ronnie's mom broke up with her latest boyfriend, and the boyfriend decided to argue with Ronnie's mom to try and get her back. The boyfriend had grabbed Ronnie's mother's long hair and was trying to pull her out of the door as she screamed! Ronnie then grabbed a cast iron frying pan off of the stove and hit the boyfriend on his head! The friend was knocked out cold!

Ronnie's mom decided to call the police. The Brunswick Police officers decided that Ronnie was trying to help his mom from being severely injured or killed. This former boyfriend had come around before trying to reason with Ronnie's mom by getting physical, cursing, and kicking in their door, etc. This time the boyfriend seemed to get the message!

Ronnie's sister, Judy, was barely fourteen years old in 8th grade, and she had run away to live with Rico, the chicken fryer, at a small establishment in town.

I called Marie, our school social worker, and let her know what was going on, She went to find Rico and Ronnie's sister, Judy.

Our school social worker took Judy back to the old Risley Middle School. It wasn't long before Judy was back with Rico again! Some teachers and a school counselor saw Judy get out of Rico's car again early in the morning before school.

When Rico was threatened with jail time, he realized that he needed to stay away from Judy and decided to leave town fast! It was too late! Judy was unknowingly pregnant with Rico's baby. About four and a half months later, she would give birth!

Ronnie told me he and his mom really worked on the old trailer. His mom was finally able to start making payments to buy the trailer instead of just renting. Ronnie confided in me that he and his mom really worked hard to make their trailer much nicer. Ronnie's mom bought wood paneling to cover the holes in the walls. She bought some nice new linoleum for the floor and put in a new window! Then they took off the door to his mom's clothes closet and installed a couple of shelves for the baby's things. He told me that the closet was big enough to put a crib in under the shelves.

Ronnie's family wasn't the only one at the middle school in which a baby had been born to a young teenage mother. One mentally handicapped boy in eighth grade special needs classes had gotten two girls pregnant at the same time and same school at Risley!

Another girl was pregnant with her second child while in eighth grade! One of the secretaries at our school bragged to everyone that her son had two girls pregnant at the same time!

I admit that at first, I was shocked when I had after school duty outside the school. I would see middle school girls walking in their new slippers and housecoats to show off their newborn babies! These were eleven to fifteen-year-old girls!

The girls were allowed six weeks of home schooling by a traveling teacher, so they wouldn't get too far behind their classmates.

In the hallway, where my class was later moved, it was not unusual to hear a loud ruckus outside the door! Girl students would start screaming, ripping fake braids out of the other girl's head, clawing with their long fake nails, breaking them off at the quick, and rolling around on the floor trying to bite each other, etc. The fight was usually over a boy who had gotten both pregnant and was having sex with both!

Several times, the music/band teacher would call for assistance outside his classroom due to the fighting female students.

I always would rather have boys in my middle school classes because girls usually brought another set of problems, which were sometimes sexual in nature.

For a few weeks, I had only one girl in my classes with my boys! She came up to me and whispered in my ear that she was really "itching down there." So, I told her to go to the bathroom right outside my room and wet some paper towels and then wash herself "down there." She continued complaining and squirming in her seat. As she walked by the boys' seats, she would slide her hands across their backs, arms, and hands.

Finally, I sent her to the school nurse. When she left my room, all my boys breathed a sigh of relief and started complaining. They told me that she kept touching and rubbing on them and smiling at them while they were trying to do their work.

My boys didn't like her in "our class." However, there was nothing that I could do. After school one day, I decided to talk to our principal about what she was doing in my class. Finally, she was charged with sexual harassment. I had to fill out the forms, and she had to go to a meeting at the Glynn County School Board. Right after that, her family moved out of the area.

Over spring break, my principal called me and told me that he had received bad news!

One of my former students, David, had been murdered by two other teenagers! All three had broken out of a psychiatric hospital for children and teens in another city in southeast Georgia. I was shocked and broke down over the phone! My student, David, had been killed by having his head bashed in with a concrete block as he was being raped by the two other boys under an overpass late at night near of Savannah.

All three young teenage boys, at the time, had run away and were hiding under an overpass when the two other boys decided to rape and kill David!

Just before spring break, David had found what looked to be a church sermon handwritten by some unknown person. David had found it in a local park in Brunswick. He treated the sermon very reverently and called the sermon "The Word of God." David told me that he wanted me to have it. So, I kept it in my briefcase as a reminder of him for many years. I still think of him every once in a while, even after all these years. Really, I don't think most of the problems David encountered were his fault. He had a difficult and short life, and mainly the trouble he got into was because he was angry about the irresponsible adults in his life.

I had another likeable boy in my class who was always well groomed and well dressed. I called his mom for a routine meeting, at least one regular education teacher and one special needs teacher must be present, and everyone who attends must sign the individual education plan (IEP) that can continue for a year. There must be at least one meeting a year to discuss with a parent how their child is progressing in the special needs' classes, as well as the regular education classes.

There can be more meetings as needed.

When his mom came to the meeting, I was surprised by how young and pretty she was. After meeting with her, I found out that she was twelve years old when her son was born. Her mother's boyfriend raped her at eleven years old and had gone to prison for that crime! However, she loved her child and did the best she could for him!

Another student I taught was quiet and calm most of the time. However, he had an explosive temper when he became upset! He kicked over a desk because of something another student had whispered to him and ran to the door trying to leave my room. I held up my right hand and asked him to stop. He pushed into me, and you could hear the ligament pop; the ligament was torn, in my hand! He ran away out the door.

I called the front office to get someone to chase him and bring him back. Our school nurse came to check on me and taped my finger. She told me that my finger was probably broken, and I would need to go to the walk-in clinic a few blocks away after school! Thank goodness that was the last class of the day! I had to wear a metal finger stall and brace for about four to five weeks!

The school pressed charges against my student and his mother had him moved to another special education teacher's class!

Once, while Ryan, a 6th grader, was trying to solve a math problem on the board, another student started making fun of him because I complimented his board work. So, Ryan made threats to the other guy doing the taunting. Then Carlos jumped up in front of me, trying to get to Ryan. While Ryan could make wisecracks, etc., he would not get into a physical altercation with anyone, even though he was bigger than most of my other students.

The next thing I knew, all three of us were knocked down with Ryan under my backside, and Carlo was whaling away on top of me trying to get Ryan! The classroom door was kicked open, and all three of us went down the three wooden steps upside down to the concrete sidewalk!

A male teacher in another building saw us through a window and ran down the long hall and out the door! Thank goodness! The other teacher, Mr. Clay, had told one of his students to call the office for help! Mr. Clay was able to grab the boys off me as they continued to fight! I almost had my shirt torn off, and I was tired and upset to say the least!

All of us had scrapes and bruises! Each boy was suspended and had to have their parents come to school to meet with the guidance counselor, principal, assistant principal, social worker, and their emotional behavioral disorders teacher, and me; I was NOT happy! This would happen anytime my students got into trouble at school.

This was called a suspension committee meeting to determine if their emotional disabilities were the reason that they were unable to control themselves appropriately.

If their disability was determined to be the underlying cause of their issues that they were recently involved in, then the work that they missed would have to be provided to them, and a homeschool teacher was provided daily for a few hours.

If it was determined that their disability was not the cause of their issues, they would receive zeros for all missed work.

If the student could control their behaviors when they wanted or needed to avoid punishment, then it would be determined that they were probably oppositional/defiant disordered and should not be in an emotional/behavioral disorders special education program, but instead, in an alternative school setting.

I had another student in my class who fit the profile of oppositional/defiant disordered and was constantly causing problems in my classroom.

Tim would not listen and would constantly make fun of other students, etc. He would not follow directions or do his work. He was constantly verbally abusive, snickering at other students when they answered questions and when I praised the students who tried hard.

To alleviate this problem, a meeting was held with the appropriate staff. It was decided to drop Tim from my emotional/behavioral disorders program and place him at the alternative school.

Tim skipped classes at the alternative school often and especially in the afternoons. After lunch I had a couple of classes of eighth graders in my classroom.

Several times a week, we would catch Tim watching and listening to us and then start to make fun of my students as they were working hard.

So, that meant that I had to call the office to get him off the school property again! I was a little worried that one day he might bring a weapon, but none was ever found on him.

Before Tim had been placed at the alternative school, I had gone to visit the school, the teachers, and administration. I had even sat in on some classes where Tim would be allowed to receive an education. I especially bonded with one of the teachers, Mrs. Banks.

I went to visit a few times to determine if this was the best placement for everyone involved! I did wonder how such a sweet person could handle these unruly and rude students all day.

I found out that it took a terrible toll on her. A few months after my last visit, she died of a heart attack in her classroom at the alternative school! The pressure she was under became too much, and it killed her!

Later, my husband, Richard, and our twin daughters, Adrien and Arien, went to court due to a car accident they had recently been part of.

While they were waiting to talk to the court, the girls recognized one of my former students from Risley—Tim! The guy who kept coming around my classroom after I sent him to the alternative school.

It seemed that Tim had dropped out of the alternative education program. Now he was in court for killing small domestic animals and beating his pregnant girlfriend!

One of my favorite students, Ronnie, loved sports, especially baseball, and was a talented player. However, he could have a terrible temper. I told him several times that he needed to learn to control his temper, or he would get in a world of trouble that he wouldn't like. I don't think he really believed me, but I had told him the truth!

Then, one day it happened! Ronnie got really upset about a call the umpire made on the baseball field. Ronnie thought the umpire was wrong when a teammate of his was "out"! Ronnie tried to argue with the umpire, but he would not change the call. Ronnie got so angry that he threw a canned drink at the umpire and hit him!

Ronnie was thrown out of the game and thrown off the team for the rest of the year!

Ronnie came to my room the next morning and wanted me as his special education teacher to write a letter explaining that he was unable to control his temper. He thought he should be put back on the team.

A teammate of Ronnie's came with him for moral support because Ronnie was a star player. I hated to tell him, "No." but I did! I knew I had done the best thing for Ronnie in the long run. Ronnie was banned from the ballpark for the rest of the season!

I told him that sometimes people have to take their punishment and learn from it, and sometimes it hurts. However, I told him it was a good lesson because his teammates will also be affected by his bad decision. "You aren't just hurting yourself; you hurt your teammates, your coaches, and the umpire you hit." Ronnie stomped off to homeroom but was back in my class and on time. He was quiet for a few days, but he got over it!

Everything was not rosy in my class all the time. Of course, with middle school teenage boys, who were also diagnosed by at least one psychologist and seemed to be determined to have emotional behavioral disorders, things could get dicey quickly.

I had some of the most severely disturbed E/BD students I had ever met in my life! One student personally threatened me by saying that he wanted to kill me by ripping my liver out!

I wouldn't act upset or shocked; the students couldn't make me act scared! I would usually just laugh and tell them to get to work, or there would be no fun Friday for the ones who could not behave and couldn't control themselves. Usually, all the students who needed a math and reading class were taught by me unless they could have good behaviors in a regular classroom and were working at the correct grade level.

If the kids completed their work for the week, they could pick a snack. I would save the test, worksheets, or whatever for them to complete. No snacks, no games, etc. until work was caught up for that hour, and I meant it! Some kids would get mad because they didn't finish their work and the other kids were playing games, especially, UNO. If they had enough points, they could pick a treat from the day-old bakery. This was a great motivator for teenage boys, who always seemed to be hungry. I brought snacks for fun Friday The kids who followed the rules and completed their work were rewarded. However, for the kids that didn't follow the rules, "too bad, so sad! No snacks or time on the playground!

Yes, of course, the kids who didn't get to participate were mad, yelling, etc. I told them that when I made a promise, I would stand by it. If they wanted to be part of the fun next time, they needed to make a promise to themselves so they could participate next Friday.

A student in my class happened to be the only girl I had the first year at Risley. She would pretend that she had a gun and pull the trigger in my face during a math class to try to intimidate me so I wouldn't call on her during class.

Janet was fifteen years old in 8th grade and was at least six inches taller than me!

This was her first year back in a regular school with half a day in my classes. It was important for her to attend my classes. If she missed classes, she could be returned to the previous school. It was a school in the county for seriously mentally disturbed students.

At the previous school, she would have to earn points to do anything special outside of her severely emotionally disturbed classroom. It was a privilege to even get to eat in the school lunchroom, instead of the classroom. It was also a privilege to try to succeed in our school and my classes for a half day. I told her privately if she didn't think she could handle rules, she would have to go back. Janet was never great, but she never threatened me again.

Poor Janet did have a horrible home life in the "projects." Other teachers that knew her from years before, told me that usually she would show up at one of the Risley teachers' home at dinner time and "come to visit." They would usually give her a sandwich and a piece of fruit. The teachers who knew her felt sorry for Janet since her mother was a drug addict and a prostitute who was often gone most of the night. Sometimes they would even let Janet sleep on a blanket on the carpet in their safe homes.

Later that year, Janet graduated from Risley Middle School and went on to play basketball at Glynn Academy, a local high school. She was an outstanding player and after high school, got the opportunity to play on a traveling basketball team in Europe. She learned to control herself and make her own way while becoming independent.

Over the years, I have seen former E/BD students in town, and they always come up to me and hug me. They usually tell me that I was the best teacher they ever had! Even though at the time, they would curse me, yell at me, refuse to follow directions, and sometimes threaten to kill me!

I believe they really knew that I worried about them and cared about them and they felt safe with me. They knew what to expect of me, and they needed to vent their frustrations. Most of the adults in their lives would lie to them and forget their promises made to the kids in their care. I never forgot my promises to the kids in my care! Children learn so much from adults, and sometimes it's bad things:

One of my former students tried to rob a female cabbie in town. He was in the back seat, aiming a gun at her. She reached back, grabbed the gun from him, and almost beat him to death with it! Then, she called the police!

Another former student stole a car from behind a house. The police were called, and they caught up to him. He jumped out of the car while it was moving, and his leg was run over and broken!

Then there was the former student who wrote a note to a small restaurant on HWY 341: "This is a holdup, give me all of your money." They did, and then called the local police. He had written the note on the back of one of his mother's checks! The police had his name and address within reach! No searching necessary!

Then there was another one of my students, a fifteen-year-old boy who lived with his granddad (mom and dad were out of the picture). He grabbed his granddad's loaded gun and aimed it at him and threatened to shoot him. He demanded money and keys to the car from his grandfather. The grandfather called the police and he was arrested and assigned to the Youth Detention Center in Waycross, GA.

The boys in my class all knew what had happened and said awful things, like, "He better not bend over in the shower!"

I had a male student, Leon, at Risley who had a twin sister, Leona. She was not in special needs classes; however, Leon was for three hours daily.

It was a sad story because the twins' elderly grandparents had custody of their grandchildren. Right after the twins were born, their mother disappeared from their lives. She left them in a cheap motel room in another state, in the middle of the motel bed for several days until the housekeeper found them.

After the babies were found, the police were finally able to contact their grandparents to see if they could take their grandchildren temporarily. The grandparents continued raising them thirteen years later with no sign of their daughter, who was addicted to illegal drugs and usually worked as a prostitute to get the money for another fix. At the time when I was in contact with the family, the mother was never in the picture.

Their grandson had severe issues. However, the granddaughter seemed okay. The grandson, my student, told me, with a wild look in his eyes, that when his grandparents went to bed at night, he would wait until they went to sleep, and then sneak into their bedroom with the knife! He hated his grandmother and thought of killing her often.

Also, when they all went to church, he thought about killing their preacher and took a huge knife in his backpack with him everywhere he went.

After school that day, he opened his backpack for me and showed me a huge butcher knife. I asked him where he got the knife and wasn't he afraid to bring it to school. He said that he didn't usually take it out of his bookbag, and he knew he could trust me—his teacher!

As soon as he left for home, I had to call our principal and my student's psychologist. Just before he had left for home, he had told me that he was about ready to kill as many people in the church as he could, and I had seen the knife!

My principal came to my room and said that he had contacted the local
police. They indicated they would pick him up and take him to the hospital for evaluation.

Years later, I was putting my grocery bags in the back of my vehicle one evening, when a big African American guy rode up fast to my car on his bike. I turned quickly and was a little afraid of the young man as he grabbed and hugged me tight! Then he yelled, "Mrs. Smith!" I had not seen Leon for years! He had grown up and was over six feet by several inches. He seemed in good spirits and was happy to see me! We talked a few minutes, and then he rode away on his bike, waving at me. I haven't seen him since that unexpected encounter.

I hope his life is calm.

Afterword 1
Risley Middle School, Glynn County, Georgia

The three teachers who had filled in the last year in the emotional behaviors disorders class before I took over left no directions or reasons for their early departures! (Each teacher had only worked three months before they quit!)

I knew what they had gone through; they had lived through the turmoil, fighting, and screaming, and I had finally conquered most of the kids' hearts and stomachs!

Many of my students, who were without a father figure, were very angry! The boys had no one to teach them how to be a real man! Their father may show up occasionally at night to get money from their mother, which the family really needed for food, clothes, and utilities. Most of these men were not real men! The kids and their mothers could not count on these self-centered men! Most of these kids in my room had no real father figure to learn from! Many men had two or three women they had impregnated, and sometimes it was hard to figure out how all these kids were related.

I tried to help the kids, usually boys, as much as I could. These kids needed to have something to look forward to and depend on. So, if I said something I followed up on it!

Most of my students lived in an environment of broken promises. So, all the kids had to do was behave, follow school rules, and complete regular classwork.

My students had to carry folders to their regular classes and get them signed by their other teachers. They were all on a point system. They didn't exactly love it, but it was the best way I could keep up with them as they navigated the regular school day while they were out of my sight and out of my classroom.

The folders were a method to communicate with the regular education teachers about the students we shared.

If the students followed my rules and got their other teachers to sign and initials any problem area or give a star for good behavior, I saw it!

They had to have a certain number of points for the week and just complete a quick assignment or test for each subject. If they had enough points on Friday, they could pick a snack from my snack container for each hour they were with me.

I also had a big bottle of good lotion that the black kids especially used so they wouldn't look "ashy"! If they came to me early in the morning before school, I might trim their hair a little like they were my own sons.

Afterword 2

I asked my kids what some of their favorite snacks were and stocked up! Remember, the day-old bakery is a great place to get snack cakes, honey buns, doughnuts, moon pies, etc. Of course, most teenage boys are always hungry. So, that worked out well! Many times we would play a few hands of UNO for the ones who had completed their work during the week and had completed a short assignment on Fridays.

If the kids had not earned enough points for the week, they had to make up their work, or if they didn't make it up, they would usually pout and get mad. Then zeroes would be put in my gradebook, and there would be no treats for them!

The other kids would laugh at the sore losers; however, I would tell the rest of the class not to laugh. I would also tell the kids who had finished their work that the students who had not completed their work were already upset, and they knew that they couldn't blame anyone but themselves. So, no fun and games for them!

The regular education teachers were great about signing my kid's folders.

They said that it was a great tool to keep in touch with a minimum of time expended.

In fact, the teachers at Risley thought it was such a good idea that I only missed "Teacher of the Year" by a couple of votes my first year. That was also my first year of teaching middle school boys, and I was very proud of that!

Years later, Ronnie showed up at our house while he was working for a pool company. My husband called me out and asked if I knew who this guy was. It was Ronnie! He told me the only thing that really "took the chip off of his shoulder" was when he went in the United States Marine Corps. He said after doing thousands of pushups and sit-ups, he finally let go of his anger! I was proud of him! He had a nice haircut and was wearing a nice, clean uniform. I went over to Ronnie and told him that I was proud of him, and then I hugged him with tears in my eyes!

Chapter 7
Foreword

Golden Isles Elementary School, Brunswick, Georgia

After three years at Risley Middle School, I decided I needed a break from the middle school environment (6th–8th grade). I especially needed a break from the teenage boys with severe emotional issues. I had enjoyed a lot of the students in my classes, and I was proud and happy to see them starting to gain more confidence in themselves as they were learning.

My principal wanted me to stay especially since I had made it through three school years and rarely took a sick day. The three teachers before me only stayed three months each! I probably had set a record!

I knew where my heart really was—with the elementary specific learning disabled, and the higher functioning mentally disabled children!

I was excited! I really liked the teachers who I would closely be working with, not only the special education teachers, but the regular education teachers as well as the principal and vice principal! I learned that since the principal's first name was Ken and the vice principal was a cute and stylish woman, they were called "Ken and Barbie," like the dolls, out of earshot, but all in fun!

Since I had survived middle school while I taught the EBD students at Risley, the special needs teacher at Golden Isles wanted me to teach the fourth and fifth graders (EBT).

The special education team had a terrible disagreement! As we were trying to set schedules for each special education teacher, I realized that I was going to teach all the third, fourth, and fifth grade EBD (emotional behavioral disordered) kids with multiple hours. That meant the kids with EBD would still only be in my special needs classroom. I didn't mind some EBD kids, but I really didn't just want all EBD kids because I needed a little break.

I at least needed a couple of groups of the 4th and 5th grade specific learning-disabled students! That's why I had left Risley. I really had enjoyed and worried about most of my students; however, I was worn down! I had been through a lot of emotions when my male student was raped and killed, and some students who couldn't seem to understand right from wrong who had to wear ankle bracelets and had to stay in my room all day! I needed a break. I didn't want to have to be tough all day long; sometimes I wanted to laugh and have fun with my students, and I was a teacher who was tired of having to be tough all...day...long!!

I didn't mind some emotional/behavioral disordered kids, and I had agreed to team teach with a regular education teacher for two hours a day. The first hour I taught English/writing skills. I walked across the hall to Mrs. Jackson's regular education fourth grade class, and she would help me. Then, Mrs. Jackson taught the reading class, and I would assist her. It was a way to help students and teachers get to know each other better and help the students more. Next year, we taught the same students in fifth grade, still for two hours daily. I thought it was a great idea. So, we both would get to know our students well.

Everyone wanted me to teach all the emotional/behavioral disordered kids. I had let my E/BD certification lapse, but still had my specific learning disabilities and mental retardation certificates. I could teach E/BD students but, could not be the only SPED teacher. I didn't want to go back to college to recertify at the time.

A couple of county administrators for special education who I knew from teaching at Risley Middle School came to our rescue! My new principal and assistant principal, who were both guidance counselors, and all the special needs teachers sat in on the meeting in a large conference room at Golden Isles Elementary.

Everyone was allowed time to state their opinions about how the classes should be set. Then, the next thing I knew, I was the new special education lead teacher.

I had just gotten out of a rough situation with my emotional/behavioral disorders boys at Risley Middle School. I really didn't want extra work, especially since I was new to the school. I wanted to make friends and not come across as a "know-it-all." Whatever I said, hit on deaf ears! Mrs. Lakes, the special education coordinator for Glynn County, was happy! She had seen what I had accomplished at Risley Middle School. In my last year at Risley, I had become the team leader of the special education teachers and SPED paraprofessionals. Then, during my last year at Risley, I was asked to check the other SPED teachers' individual education plans (IEP's) before they were forwarded to the county office. If there were mistakes, I discussed it with the teacher in question to help them make corrections. Of course, some teachers were better than others when writing the IEPs. I was compensated for the extra work.

From that bad beginning at Golden Isles Elementary, things began to become more manageable and made a lot more sense!

I received a stipend in my monthly check at Golden Isles for being the team leader. Once a month I had the same substitute in my classroom all day for the year. Since my substitute was in college to become a teacher, he gained a great deal of experience with special needs students and kids in general.

If any SPED teachers needed help between 8:00 and 11:00 a.m., such as needing me to make a change in one of their students, IEP like changing the hours a child was served, updating, adding or deleting something, etc. I made myself available. To make a change in a student's IEP, one of the parents would have to be notified in time to come to the meeting.

In addition, I would get requests to complete an observation of a child and I was able to do that. Those three hours would fill up fast!

At 11:00 a.m., I had to be in my car on my way to attend a meeting with all the other lead teachers in the county. Most of the time, we would go to local restaurants where we could talk and eat with friends from other schools. We could ask questions and find out more information. Sometimes our students would move out of our school zone and into another. Then, if we knew where they had moved, we could take our teacher folder to the new lead teacher.

Our special education administrator would always have new information for us to digest and discuss. We received new materials we had ordered for our team members.

I was so happy that I was back in elementary school! I really enjoyed teaching at Golden Isles Elementary. At the time, most of the students were low-to-middle income kids who mainly lived close to the school. Most kids were nice country kids, and their parents wanted them to do their best and tried to help their children the best they could.

In the mornings, before the bell rang, it was fun for me to watch the children riding their bikes to school, and sometimes their parents would ride along on their own bikes just to keep an eye on their children to make sure they made it safely to school. Some of the mothers would be pushing a special stroller for fast walking and even jogging.

Parents almost always showed up for important meetings about their children. The Parent Teacher Association (PTA) meetings were always packed. I found out that the teachers and paraprofessionals always stood in the back of the seated crowd of parents and other family members, so we could make a quick exit to our rooms when we were released by our principal. I had never seen so many family members! It was fun and exciting to meet the parents of my students and to know that they cared about their children's education!

We had cute twin sisters in special classes in specific learning disabilities classes due to reading and written language issues. Their older brother had emotional issues and was also served through the special education programs in emotional/behavioral disorders.

Their mother had her own demons with her drug addiction. She would be out on bail for a while, then gone again, back to jail. Sometimes she would give me money to keep for her children's future field trips, etc. So, I would put the money in a marked envelope and store it in the locked office safe. She would always tell me that even if she begged me for her money, don't give it to her! Then she would show up again, crying and begging for the money that she had given me!

For a few weeks, she even had a job at a local carwash but quit because "the job took too much of her free time!" She complained to me, an overworked special education teacher! I commiserated with her; however, I thought it was funny complaining to me! I thought of the old saying, "You have to walk in their shoes to really understand!"

The twins always seemed clean and dressed in clean clothes; however, I couldn't get over the fact that the girls seemed to keep head lice most of the time! Head lice spreads quickly when near other people. So, I called their mother and got permission to use lice shampoo on their hair at school. We had two special education para pros that volunteered to treat the girls' hair and then comb out the dead lice and eggs that were glued onto the hair shafts. Probably the school funded the shampoo from the money that we made from the teachers' cold drink machines and snack machines. Someone else bought a nice hair dryer. It was awful, but I found out that you must comb out all the nits (eggs), and that is usually a long and tedious job!

I would like to say that was the end of the story, but it wasn't. If all the bedding, towels, couch pillows, bedspreads, carpets, and stuffed animals, etc. at home weren't treated, the girls would probably have lice again! And, of course, they did!

Lice is easily spread to other children and even adults. I have seen kids scratching their heads, and I would quietly go up to them as they worked and looked at their scalps, and it would look like a baseball game going on in their hair! There would be so many lice that it would make me quietly shiver. Of course, the child would have to be sent home and get treated before they could come back to school.

I had a great placement of my room next door to the nurse's office and just across the hall from the principal's office!

I had a fourth-grade boy in my class who constantly sucked yellow-green mucus back up his nose instead of using a tissue and blowing it out. It had become a bad habit. He would be working at his desk, and you could hear him trying to suck it back up. The other students even complained of the sickening sound!

I bought Jack his own box of tissue to put on his desk and a small plastic trash can to keep by his chair.

I had him see our school nurse. She explained to him that when he had the urge, blow as much mucus out as possible into a tissue instead of sucking it back into his nasal passages.

The other kids in my class hated hearing the sucking noise for two hours a day!

Finally, I decided to call his mother, Candy Cotton, who danced at the "local gentlemen's club" in town. I called his mom because I was worried about Jack's infected sinus cavities.

His mother said that he was always like that and didn't seem worried. I suggested that she take him to the doctor or at least talk to our school nurse. While he was at Golden Isles, she never took him to the doctor. The social worker visited his mother to discuss how dangerous this could be to her son's health.

Jack was withdrawn from school, and we never saw him again! I hope he got medical treatment somewhere!

One day, my principal, Dr. Wills, called me into his office and asked my thoughts on what kind of punishment I would suggest for a new student. "Well," I said." What did he do?"

Dr. Wills said, "Well, Sammy was jumping off the lunchroom tables, pretending he was Superman!" He acts like he only has half a brain.

"Well, Dr. Wills, I'm not sure if anyone has told you yet, but since it is confidential on a need-to-know basis only! He has a gifted brother enrolled at this school. However, Sammy was not so lucky…he was born with only one-half of a brain! I have seen the brain scans on the left side of his head; he has a brain. However, on the right side of his head, there is only fluid!"

Poor Dr. Wills turned very pale! He didn't know what to think or say! I had really surprised him with my answer! However, it was true!

Dr. Wills decided that I should determine Sammy's punishments from then on since he was in my special education classes!

Another interesting family was a divorced mother with two cute and always well-dressed emotionally disturbed boys. I had recently noticed that when their mother came to get her sons, she had started dressing differently. She was now wearing lots of makeup with false eyelashes, see-through blouses with a colorful bra underneath, and tight short shorts with high spike heels.

Then one day, while I was waiting for her to come to my room and get the boys, the oldest boy told me that his mom was now a movie star!

His mom would take the boys with her when she went to her boyfriend's house! The kids would watch a big TV in the living room while their mom and her boyfriend (a producer) filmed movies in the back part of the house!

I wrote a report about this for the social worker who was assigned to our school at the time. I never found out any more information about what was going on. I was worried about the boys who had both been sexually molested by an uncle and had been in counseling for several years and were still on medication.

A sad, but, at the same time, funny incident occurred when I was giving a Friday spelling test to third graders. Most of the time, I would call the word and then come up with a sentence using the word in question. This time, I didn't have a chance. The word was "pole." Before I could say the sentence, my school phone rang, and as I hung up the phone, one of my students said, "Pole, what is that?" Another student trying to be helpful answered him: "You know, like when my Momma dances on a "pole" where she works!" Then, the other little boy said, "Oh, yeah!"

I didn't know whether to laugh or cry! And yes, his mother was also a pole dancer at the local "gentlemen's club" in Brunswick!

There were a lot of strange incidents at the front of the school and across from the main school office where my room was located.

Many times, there would be a familiar car engine stop, and then I would hear the mother get out of her car. I heard the mother chastise her two special needs boys on the way into the school.

Too often the oldest boy would climb on the roof of his mother's SUV and just stand up there. Mom and Dad were divorced, and she was the most "stable" parent to raise the boys. I assumed. Although sometimes I would come out of a supermarket and see one of the boys walking around on the hood and the other boy on the roof of their vehicle, even at a grocery store parking lot. Maybe she made the kids go with her, so at least they couldn't destroy her home while she went shopping!

Sometimes, the secretary of the school would call me on the intercom to find me before school. I would have to go to the front of the school to grab the oldest boy off Mom's car roof or hood. So then other parents could drive up to the front doors and let their children get out safely and securely. There were times when the oldest son was so obstinate and unyielding to his mom's requests to just get out of the vehicle and go inside the school that he sometimes had his mother in tears. I had to grab him off the car so mom could go to work! It didn't matter what she said to her boys! I think her sons thought that it was all their mom's fault that Daddy had to leave their home, and they were trying to punish their mother. Every time I met with the parents, the boy's dad seemed to come across as calm and relaxed. However, the mother, who was raising the two sons, always seemed stressed and upset.

Golden Isles always had quite a few parents who let their children out by the front doors of the school. I didn't mind opening car doors for the kids. However, many times when I would open the car doors, all kinds of garbage would fall out onto the school driveway.

There was no trash can by the school doors, so I would just pick it up and throw it back into the car! Usually, the trash in the back of some of the cars would continue to build until the kids' legs were covered up almost to their knees! I couldn't understand it! I would be worried that there were all kinds of vermin and parasitic creatures hiding in the trash! Sometimes I would even spot roaches in the garbage with the kids and knock them off the car seats!

Thinking of vermin, we had a very disturbing incident with one of our special needs eight-year-old boys. He would come to my room for an hour a day to participate in a reading group at his level.

Jasper was a cute and sweet little boy who was paralyzed from the waist down. So, that meant that he had to wear diapers all the time under his clothes. One day I kept noticing baby roaches running around in my room.

The school was sprayed often, so I never saw a roach in my room!

Finally, I realized that little roaches were coming out of his backpack, hanging on the back of his wheelchair! I took him out of his wheelchair and there were live roaches sitting on his seat and diapers!

When I took him to the school nurse, next door to my room, she noticed that his diaper was so wet and soggy; she didn't think he had been changed since the last diaper change just before the bus took him home the afternoon before. Poor Jasper! His mother had not even changed him recently!

No wonder Jasper always seemed to have terrible diaper rash! It almost looked like his diaper area had been burned! The social worker was called and took pictures of the raw looking flesh in his diaper area. She then went to talk to his mother about the infected looking rash in Jasper's diaper area and all the roaches in his backpack and wheelchair. Our social worker asked the special education paraprofessionals to mark his diapers when they changed him.

His mom didn't want to lose custody because she wanted the money that Jasper brought in every month!

The other special needs teacher who worked with Jasper helped me take the wheelchair totally apart and spray it with roach spray. Finally, all the roaches were dead and gone! Then we put the parts of the wheelchair in hot water with good detergent, rinsed it, and left it to dry in the sun most of the day. We got it back together and sent Jasper home on the bus in his wheelchair, which was nice and clean again! This time we marked his diaper to make sure he had a fresh one on in the morning. The reason that a wet diaper didn't bother him is because he was paralyzed from the waist down!

How did we have all this time to take care of Jasper? We had a very good school nurse and wonderful paraprofessionals who would jump in to help as needed!!

Linda was another one of my students; she was very poor and lived in an old beat-up shack in Brunswick. Her mother had already raised a family, and now her grown children were raising children as well.

Linda's mom had a second-generation family with at least four more children in elementary school. Linda's mom didn't have a car, so she would have to pay a friend to drive her to Golden Isles Elementary when there were meetings that she had to attend. I remember that Mrs. Johns, the teacher right across from my room, whom I taught with daily for two hours, also had one of Linda's sisters, Pam. Pam was not in a special needs class and was an average student. Mrs. Johns was a little nervous trying to talk with Linda's mother and her friend. Neither one would say a word, but sometimes I could get Linda's mom to talk if I bragged on Pams progress. Pam was a pretty good writer and reader in the classes that we shared together.

One day, when Linda (Pam's sister across the hall) came into my room early, she matter-of-factly told me that her father had been killed with a knife in a bar fight last night. I asked her why someone killed him. Then she said that her father had said something about another man's girlfriend!! I was shocked and felt bad for her! However, she did tell me that she didn't see him often and he didn't live with her family!

Mrs. John broached the subject of starting a school newspaper based on our writing and reading classes. Our principal loved the idea, gave us copy paper, and had the paraprofessionals copy and staple copies for the entire school! At the time, we had around 750–800 students. The newspaper was usually six to eight pages and was a big hit! All the classrooms started sending in poems, short stories, and original art! We had find-a-words, jokes, and some relevant dates in history. The paper was very well received, and we started getting a plethora of items to put in our classroom/school newspaper! Since I had been the editor of the high school newspaper at King High School in Tampa, Florida, I pretty much knew what I was doing and loved it!

I was also on the leadership team and co-chaired for several years. Usually, a small group would travel to Athens, Georgia, where the leadership program was based at the University of Georgia and led by two UGA professors.

Occasionally, if I was going alone, my husband, Richard, would travel with me, and while I was attending meetings, Richard would check out bookstores, sports stores, etc. Then, when we broke for lunch, we would go to cute cafes, etc. Then after the meeting was over for the day, we would go to dinner at a nice restaurant. Of course, my mileage and fuel bill, hotel bill, and my food bill were covered by the Glynn County School System.

Also, I traveled with another teacher to schools around the state of Georgia to consult and conduct workshops about developing a leadership team for their own schools.

The principal and assistant principal were both onboard with Golden Isles Elementary having a real functioning leadership team. The downtown school board paid the yearly fees for our school and fees while we traveled.

The principal and assistant principal didn't decide everything that we did as a school community. Of course, they had to pay the bills and make sure the curriculum was being taught correctly at each grade level. Each grade level was required to teach so many minutes per day. The lower grades usually had a recess built into their schedules and occasionally the upper grades did as well.

Teachers at the same grade level taught the same subjects at the same time. This helped with scheduling time for students receiving special education services, etc.

We would vote on other items, such as if we were going to raise money by selling the popular professionally made cookie dough, gift wrap, etc.

Also, we were asked to vote on special days, such as having art day (which most kids loved), it was fun, the school would have stations set up around the school, outside and inside the school, plus math day and even science day.

Probably, the most popular days were field days. It was fun; parents would come to help set up tents, put chalk marks on the field itself, etc. The last I heard, first, second, and third places are now out. Everyone gets a "participation" ribbon now.

Trophies and ribbons were still given for spelling bees, science, history, and social studies fairs.

Our leadership team voted to participate in the students wearing uniforms daily. We tried that for one year.) However, many parents didn't want to participate, and it caused too many problems. So, the county decided to drop the uniform issue for the next year.

By this time, I had started my education specialist degree on scholarship from Glynn County Schools. Teachers who agreed to teach at least five more years in Glynn County Schools would receive a nice pay raise when they graduated with another degree.

When I did retire, my monthly check would be based on my last five years and the education specialist degree that I would have.

I would take turns driving two nights a week with other teachers also working on getting an advanced degree. At the time, I was the only teacher I knew that was going for a specialist degree.

Sometimes teachers from other schools would call Golden Isles Elementary to find out if we had room in our vehicle for them to catch a ride to Georgia Southern University

Dear Mrs. Smith

for a class. I was fine with someone new coming with us if we had room.

We always left the school at 2:45 p.m. right after the bell. Since we had a two-hour drive to get to our 5:00 p.m. class we usually made a quick stop at a burger place along the way and ate as we drove. There wasn't much time to waste; we had to drive two hours to Georgia Southern to make it on time. Then, we would rush to our different classes.

We returned to Golden Isles Elementary School around 9:00 p.m., and everyone would get in their respective vehicles and start their drive back to their own homes and families. If we hurried, we could usually all make it home by 9:30 p.m. and be in bed by 10:00 p.m., and back at school on time the next morning!

Sometimes, I took two classes, so that meant four nights a week, and the classes would be from 5:00 to 7:00 p.m., or I took two classes only two nights a week, and the classes would be from 5:00 to 7:00 p.m., then 7:00 to 9:00 p.m., and if we hurried, we could still get into bed by 11:00 to 11:30 p.m. I would still have to get up and be back at school the next morning, at least at 7:30 a.m.

I still found others who wanted to share rides. Sharing rides made the time go by faster as we would discuss all kinds of subjects about school and our families.

Finally, in the summer, I took turns driving to Savannah, which was one and a half hours each way to a small outpost campus with another Glynn County teacher who taught at another Glynn County school. We traveled two to three times a week for most of the summer.

On our last day of summer classes, we both finished with classes for our degrees! We both only had to complete our final independent research and then conduct our experiments in the fall with students. Following that, we would each separately go back to Statesboro to discuss and defend our findings. So, we celebrated, by getting a delicious milkshake at a popular local ice cream shop in Savannah!

We had fun celebrating and slurping the milkshakes on the way back to Brunswick for the last time! We talked about all the free time we would now enjoy!

When school started back, I completed my final semester long project right before Christmas break!

I was amazed at how much extra time I had in the afternoons after almost two years of driving to Statesboro. My friends and colleagues could hardly believe that I had already graduated within two years while teaching fulltime. I was on the leadership team, and I had a big part in the school newspaper, and was team leader of the special education team! It was great to be done!

Rick and Robbie were identical twins, and both had autism. However, they both were brilliant in their own ways. Rick was healthier than his twin brother, Robbie, who had to take steroids from birth due to his terrible asthma.

I spoke with Mrs. Johns, who was Rick's homeroom teacher. She said she was really concerned because she didn't know much about autism disorder.

Rick would always go up to Jenna during homeroom because he would want to discuss World War II history. So, she would send him to me. He would work out intricate war plans and draw them on one of my large whiteboards and explain his plans to me. I would always agree how brilliant the plans were and how it seemed that it really might have worked!

Hindsight is 20/20. We hit on an idea of having a professor knowledgeable in World War II history. He taught and came by at the local college and visited have lunch with Rick a couple times a month.

Sometimes when there was a bad storm or a possible hurricane drawing near, Rick would want to draw a map of Florida and Georgia on one of my whiteboards and keep it there for the duration to show where it was heading that day. Rick would explain the barometer readings to me that day and explain to me what they actually meant. Rick did have a wealth of information in subjects that he enjoyed, and I loved discussing things with him.

A number of times before the morning bell rang to go to homeroom, I would have both boys in my room from around 7:40 to 8:10 a.m. Then they would go to their homerooms (they were in separate classrooms).

Robbie was also very obsessed by subject movies, even the older ones that were in the movie stores in those days. Teachers would come into my room in the mornings to talk about a certain movie with Robbie. The teachers would ask him all kinds of questions about the movie. "Who were the director and producer? Who were the main actors? What year did it come out? What was it about?" If it was on the back of the movie box, he knew it and never forgot it, according to his mother! The teachers couldn't get over it! It was fun to know that Robbie was so brilliant in movie memorabilia and loved it! If Robbie had a good week at school, their mom would take both of her boys to the movie store, and his twin brother, Rick, would check out what to watch that weekend. While Robbie would read the movie boxes and commit all the information to long term memory storage and never seemed to forget!

There was only one thing that Robbie would eat for lunch: Papa John's Pizza! I assigned one of our special education paraprofessionals to heat Robbie's pizza slice daily at lunchtime. His mom made sure that their refrigerator at home always had Robbie's favorite lunch for the week.

One day, a fourth-grade teacher was watching her students on the playground on the climbing bars, swings, etc. Then she noticed that a poor little girl in a third-grade class wasn't wearing any underpants!

Mrs. Lakes, the fourth-grade teacher, asked me to ask our social worker, Rita, to buy her some panties.

The next day, Rita brought in a cute selection of colors of underpants and gave them to the little third grade girl.

The little girl was later found wearing an old pair of underwear that belonged to her fourth-grade brother who was in Mrs. Lakes class!

When the social worker asked her what happened to her new panties, she said they were all gone! She had never even opened the packages!

The poor third and fourth grade kids usually had a strong urine smell on their bodies and clothes because all four of the kids slept together on one old mattress and two of the young kids were not yet potty trained. The kids would usually sleep in their clothes that they wore to school and would wear them for several days in a row!

The mother of the third and fourth grade children would usually send them to school in the same dirty clothes! The odor would be so strong that their teachers would have to send them to the nurse's office because she had use of a shower and washer and dryer at school!

Mrs. Lakes taught the brother of the little third grade girl with no underpants. Mrs. Lakes had recently bought a brand-new washer and dryer, so she decided to give her old washer and dryer to their mother who was coming to a special education meeting about her son. Mrs. Lakes met the children's mother, and was shocked! She had a totally different picture of the kids' mother in her mind! Instead of looking destitute, the mother had her hair professionally styled with long braids added and was wearing a beautiful red dress complete with a red jacket, red high heels, and a purse to match! She also seemed to be wearing real gold jewelry, and her long red nails seemed to be professionally done. Finally, she finished off the look with several gold teeth, false eyelashes and nice makeup!

I saw how the image of the children's mother made Mrs. Lakes change her mind about the washer and dryer! Her children always looked and smelled bad. However, their mother looked ready to go out on the town! I really couldn't blame Mrs. Lakes! The mother of the four poor children certainly didn't treat them right like a loving parent should and would!

I had a cute fifth grade student in my class. Freddy had freckles across his nose, usually wore a crew cut, and was always talking about fishing at the river and swimming.

Freddy came into my classroom at lunch time as usual, so he could get a little extra help with his reading skills. We called this time "lunch and read." He had a real reading and written expression deficit.

Our guidance counselor, Mrs. C. N., had talked me into having him come during his fifth-grade lunch time.

Next thing I knew, Freddy was telling me a story about what had happened at the river last weekend. It seemed that the kids were playing around in the river when one kid stepped in a hole and swallowed a lot of water.

Next, Freddy told me that the adults had walked away to start packing up to go home. So, it was up to Freddy to help his friend out, and he knew his friend was choking under water and would die if he didn't save his friend soon! Finally, Freddy was able to maneuver his friend's foot and leg from under a tree root and got him to safety!

When the adults heard the commotion, they all turned toward the river, realizing what was going on. Freddy was the hero for the day!!

I questioned him a little more and decided to talk to a school resource officer without letting Freddy know. A couple of weeks later, it was Honors Day, and Freddy's parents were there without Freddy knowing!

Freddy had never gotten anything on Honors Day. However, this time he was the most important honoree! He had saved a friend's life! Freddy was the hero of that Golden Isles Elementary School Honors Day! I imagined it was quite a shock for Freddy because he had never gotten an award for anything in school before!

Freddy was red with embarrassment about being called up on stage by our school resource officer and receiving a medal and a trophy for saving a friend's life! It would probably be the biggest day in his entire school life!

That same year, and in the same 4th to 5th grade hall, I was team teaching with a fourth-grade regular education teacher. Since I had seven fourth graders with a specific learning disability in reading and reading comprehension, it worked out great.

I especially loved one chapter of their 4th grade reading textbook. It was about Lake Okeechobee and the locks (which are like gates) that must be opened to travel through the huge lake in South Florida. It is a very important lake for the residents who live in south

Florida because that is where the freshwater comes from. There are no freshwater wells in the ground in south Florida as well as the Florida Keys. All the water in the lower part of Florida comes from Lake Okeechobee by water pipes attached to the bridges. Since I had fished on the huge lake when I was a child and had friends who lived there, I thought it was really fascinating; however, the kids not so much!

One day I heard the regular fourth grade teacher call out, "Shy Passion! Pay attention and learn something new!" That was a first for me! I had never heard a girl named "Shy Passion!" I really enjoyed my time at Golden Isles Elementary School and loved my students and teachers I worked with daily.

Over the years, we saw many changes in special education classes, mainly due to the law that went into effect called "Least Restrictive Environment," which was mostly a positive change.

Most children were able to participate in their own grade level homerooms, lunch, and special classes for art, music, and physical education. Students could participate in some grade level classes. Sometimes a special education paraprofessional might be needed to accompany the student or students. However, that was not the norm.

What was great was some students would leave their homeroom classes for something like a speech/communication class several times a week for thirty to forty-five minutes at a time. Usually, the younger learning-disabled students would leave their homeroom class for one to three hours per day, every day. However, all the special education teachers tried their best to schedule their qualifying students with the least impact to their normal school day. Sometimes, the special education teacher would have enough students in a certain grade level that they could "push in" or go into the regular education classroom where some of the students had learning disabilities in reading and written language. Usually, the regular education teacher would want me to present English and written language skills especially in the fourth and fifth grades. So, we would break into small groups. According to the class size, we would usually have four to five small groups in a two-hour period. The regular education teacher set the timer, and it worked out well!

By the spring of the school year, most fifth grade students could write a pretty good five paragraph essay/report.

We could work on different types of genres. We would use social studies activities that were grade level appropriate or material from their grade level reading materials. Since I loved to write anyway, I loved working on the fifth-grade level in an average reading/writing class.

Remember, I worked with every student in the classroom daily in small groups on writing a paper on a certain topic. The regular grade level teacher read and worked with the students to glean the most important information in the selection every day.

The students who had special needs in the teacher's class could have a disability in communication skills, reading, and/or writing.

Sometimes I worked with regular education students who were originally speakers of another language. I admit it, I still miss teaching...sometimes! It was great to see a student grasp the points I was trying to convey and see them grow in their writing skills! Amazing! When the students were proud of their budding writing skills, I was usually prouder than they were!

On another subject completely, our guidance counselor was told by our social worker that some women in the community were paying a "special needs" man to have sex with them! Why? So hopefully they would give birth to a "special needs" child or children and get a monthly check for each "special" child born!!

I never found out if the crazy women's plans worked. Let's just hope not! What a horrible, self-centered plan! However, I do know that we had parents of seven children, and five were found to be special needs children. Also, the guidance counselor and others would fill their backpacks for the weekend with nonperishables: cereal, peanut butter, cheese and crackers, and fruit and breakfast bars. No one ever thanked the school for giving all that food to them. By Monday, their backpacks were empty!

Our guidance counselor also told me that she received several calls from mothers to see how they could get their child or children in special needs classes. When the counselor looked up their test scores and report card grades, she asked the mothers why they thought their child or children should be in special needs classes. They would invariably say that they needed money for a newer car and to pay some bills.

Nothing about their children's education!

When I was teaching down the long fifth grade hall and teachers and parents would drop by just to chat for a few minutes, I always tried to quickly get them into my room and away from my heavy wooden door! Partly because of the accident that Adrien, one of my twins, had in first grade that cut part of her finger off.

I talked with Mrs. Parker and asked her why she had thrown Jamie into my room so often during morning announcements.

She told me that she had to have quiet time to hear the announcements, and all her students were given a half sheet of paper and had to correct the mistakes in the sentences and complete the math problems. Mrs. Parker said that Jamie wouldn't even try to attempt the work and would just make spit balls or paper airplanes and get the whole class in an uproar!

I asked her to send him over to my room right after she took roll. Then I gave him something to do until homeroom was over and send him on his way to first period. Problem solved!

I had a female student on my special needs list that always wore boys' clothes and even boys' shoes and sport socks. She walked like a boy and really wanted to be a boy. She was allowed to play on mainly boys' baseball teams and was a great player even though she was smaller than most of the boys.

Jody was in my special needs program because she wouldn't read and write even though she was now in fourth grade. I started picking her up during homeroom. Even though I was in Mrs. John's room for two hours daily, now I knew why Jody wouldn't participate; she was too embarrassed to try in front of other kids!

I purchased several sports books for younger children, and at first Jody acted like she didn't care and wouldn't even look at the books. However, she finally opened a book or two and started asking me some words. Then, she would slam the book closed and just sit there. So, I started reading the books out loud about baseball, football, track and field, etc. Since there were only the two of us in my room at the time, Jody would sometimes try to sound out simple words using a chart on my table! I knew that she really wanted to be able to read; she was really embarrassed that she needed extra help, but I told her everyone needs help with some things!

From that simple beginning, she started standing at my door before I even got down the hall, and sometimes she had a book that she wanted to read about sports and later animals, etc.

She still wasn't a fabulous reader; however, since she was dyslexic, she was slower and had to sometimes sound out the words, but she was reading!

Later, Jody was able to go to college with a tutor provided because of her disability. She had decided that she wanted to become a Marine Corps officer after completing college. She passed the physical with 100%, plus she ran track in college and played softball.

However, she was a small person in stature and didn't get along well with the other female officer recruits in training and finally dropped out of the Marine Corps Officer training program just before graduating. The last I heard about her; Jody had become a police officer in the area and was doing well.

One of my poor little girls, Lilly, was in fourth grade and was in my classroom for the last two classes of the day. When it was time to go back to her homeroom and get ready to go on the bus, Lilly would try to linger in my classroom! One day I had to call our principal, Dr. Wills, to get her out from under my desk. She would not budge! I was worried about her and was afraid that she might be scared because she may have been sexually abused. Dr. Wills finally got her out from under the desk and walked her to the bus.

I had no real evidence, only that she never wanted to go home. She always wanted to stay with me! She would sometimes start crying if I made her leave my room to go home. She had matted fuzzy hair, and her skin was "ashy" looking. So, I tried to keep lotion for all the black kids that I taught. One day, I even asked a paraprofessional to comb out her hair, put some hair oil on it, braid it, and put little colored rubber bands on the braids to help keep it nice. She did a wonderful job, and I could tell that Lilly loved it! Lilly would hardly talk to anyone in my room, not even me.

I talked to our school social worker about Lily, and she went for a visit a couple of days later to try to talk to her mother. The mother was not home.

The social worker would sometimes pop in to try to catch Lily's mother at home to talk about Lily's hesitancy to get on the bus and not wanting to go home. However, she never could catch Lily's mother; it was if Lily's mother didn't want to talk to our social worker! How could the mother of Lily aways be gone every time our social worker dropped by? Even when she sent a letter to her mother to make an appointment, it was never acknowledged!

Over the years, if I was in a full-sized classroom, I would usually end up with another special education teacher in the room with me and her class as well. However, sometimes the other teacher or I would go into a regular education teacher's classroom and team teach, which was great for all the students and teachers.

One teacher who I shared a room with had diabetes. She went to a local palmist to talk about her sugar diabetes and thought she had real knowledge about the disease, and the palmist knew more than the doctors!

At first, she had followed her doctor's orders and gave herself shots twice a day at school: early in the morning, then after lunch time, and two more shots later in the late afternoon and late evening.

The teacher trusted the palmist more than the doctors and quit taking her shots and didn't tell me because she knew that I would have said something to our nurse about stopping her shots!

After one day without her insulin shots, she had to be rushed to our local hospital by ambulance because she was almost comatose!

Another idea that she had that was a little off center was that she, her two daughters, and her boyfriend were going to live "off the grid," and they were saving money by buying a gas refrigerator! Not only she, but one of her daughters had diabetes! The other daughter had rheumatoid arthritis and sometimes had to use a wheelchair.

This teacher also thought about going to live on another planet. Finally, she thought she and her two daughters could leave planet Earth and live somewhere else, like the people out west that poisoned themselves and put silver dollars on their closed eyes and a purple sheet on themselves. Those people had been convinced that they would somehow go to another planet or dimension and live!

There was another teacher who had married her boyfriend from college. She had a baby with him. Her mother raised the little girl while her daughter finished college, taught school, and dated guys over the years. Her long-ago boyfriend never knew about their baby! He hardly ever saw her child over the many years that had passed. Her daughter now actually lives in another state!

The teacher had recently reconnected with her boyfriend and married him but would not live with him full time. She would spend the weekend with him occasionally, where he lived in Savannah, Georgia. She often came to my room after school to talk about her situation. She told me that I gave her hope that they could be together one day for the rest of their lives! I hope I did help her.

After teaching in Vancouver, Washington, for several years and coming back to one of my favorite schools, Golden Isles in Georgia, I found out that I would have to divide my full-sized classroom into two classrooms. The reason was because another teacher would be moving in.

Mr. Causie was a nice older guy who came from another school in the county and really didn't want to teach anymore, so he didn't!

He would quietly read his Bible most of the day, and I had to share my room with him! My kids would get up and tell me what his kids were doing. Also, he didn't care what the students did, but I was upset! It wasn't fair to all our students! He would be oblivious to what his students were doing, or maybe just pretending to be oblivious to what was going on around him! He was still getting a monthly check for teaching when he wasn't doing anything for his students!

Mr. Causie would let his students go into closets with supplies that I had ordered out of MY budget for projects for all our students to use correctly. Since I team taught in fifth grade, I would sometimes be in another teacher's classroom. While I was gone, all kinds of craziness would break loose! He would let his kids go into MY closet and get a big gallon bottle of white glue and pour it on their desktops and make designs in it instead of teaching them! The youngest class of students that Mr. Causie had were third graders with a specific learning disability. That meant the students had a normal IQ and were at grade level in some subjects and usually around two years below in reading and writing skills.

If I had a class in the room during the same time he was there, I had to discipline his students so my kids could hear what was going on.

I advised of the our principal of the situation and he began monitoring him. After that, he was clearly pressured to retire. He was an old guy, but he was NOT teaching! So, he retired. He was probably glad about it!

My second year after returning from Vancouver, Washington, was a much calmer and happier year. However, I had a serious issue come up about the end of year testing. One of my 5th grade special needs students, who had a moderately low IQ, started telling students or adults that he knew he was going to pass the end of the year fifth grade test.

What test? "The one all the students in the county and state must take at grade level." The regular fifth grade teacher asked, "How do you know for sure?"

My student said, "Because Mrs. Smith gave me and the other fifth graders in her classroom all the answers!" He really did seem confident! At the time, I had just walked into a fifth grade where I team taught with a regular education teacher. Now, all her students were quiet and staring at me! I knew this was serious business, and I could lose my teaching certificate and not teach again.

I couldn't understand why he was so positive that he had passed. Our principal said she was going to have to call the superintendent of Glynn County Schools, and there would have to be an investigation about the student's allegations of cheating. Then as I walked into her office, I remembered that I had one of our special education paraprofessionals test him one-on-one, like we did for several of our special children who had a difficult time paying attention in a large room of students.

Our principal called the paraprofessional in question and confirmed that she indeed tested the student one-on-one. Thank goodness! What a mess! My student was referring to the sample questions that came up on the Smart Board! I did the same thing that the other teachers were advised to do, and that was to get the students more comfortable with test taking! I truly think that my student didn't understand what we were doing on the Smart Board! He failed fifth grade even with a tutor going to his home three afternoons a week and two hours at a time. So, he had to attend summer school and still didn't pass. I never saw him again; I found out that his family had moved to another county for his mother's job.

I had two brothers that both had to have their IEPs updated. However, I could not get either mother or father on the phone to come to school for a meeting. I also mailed two letters to their address about a meeting for both boys. Still, there was no answer. So, I asked the principal's secretary to be on the lookout for the boys' mother. Finally, one day their mother did show up, and the secretary called me. I asked her to stall to keep her there until I arrived. The mother of the boys acted like she was in a hurry. I was too! I had my folders about her sons, and I made it to the front office before she got away! The mother was surprised because she had just dropped something off for her kids. I stood in front of her large black vehicle so she couldn't go unless she ran me down! I told her that I needed her to sign some paperwork for change of a placement for the younger boy and continued placement for the older boy. She indicated that she was in a hurry. I handed my black pen to her, and she signed both documents! I told her we had made some changes in the IEPs in hours and placement. She said, "That's fine, I've gotta go!" Thank goodness; she had just gotten out of jail again for shoplifting. As she went flying down the school driveway and into the street, I stood there thinking what a role model she was for her children!! Then I went back into the school, thanked our great secretary, and walked back to my room.

Right after my encounter with their mother, our female assistant principal went downtown in search of the boys' father's small business. When she found it, there were a couple of old guys sitting around inside, but no father. Our assistant principal was gutsy! She walked into another small room and started opening closet doors, and there, the boys' father was hiding in a closet!

The boys' father said he was getting some supplies and didn't hear her! Yeah, right! It was totally ridiculous! He also signed the papers to move his youngest son to a small room at the alternative school.

These two brothers were very disrespectful to the girls and women in the fourth-grade hall including teachers and paraprofessionals. The fourth-grade brother would swagger as he walked down the halls. He even told the teachers that he "could teach them about being with a real man!" He would whistle at them in the hall and try to touch them! He was only eleven years old!!

He was moved to a small, empty room at the alternative school, but was not actually in the alternative population. His parents didn't want to deal with him, so he at least lost his audience!

I went over to his small classroom a few times to check on his special education paraprofessional, who had to be with him all day at. She had a wall phone connected to the front office that she could call for help as needed.

We would get his work together for the week, and one of our paraprofessional would pick it up. It was a pain; however, he needed to be kept away from the elementary school and other students.

When he and his older brother were together in the hallways and breakfast and lunch time, it was crazy! They both would swagger and make "catcalls" and whistle at the women they saw.

However, when the older brother was by himself, not so much. He knew that he didn't want to go to the school where his brother now was.

Let's just say we got his attention!

Then there was an overweight boy in my classroom, who became angry with me when I told him that his computer time was up. He started yelling at me and started flipping over desks and bookcases and throwing books at me.

I calmly got behind my desk and reached for my wall phone. He saw me trying to call the office and ran at me and the phone, which he was trying to tear off the wall as he beat me with it.

Finally, I yelled to a student in my room to go find our male gym coach. Until I told my student to get help, all children were stunned and just stood there with huge eyes and open mouths! I yelled to the poor kids to go to the other empty room.

The next thing I knew, our male gym coach was grabbing the student off me! The broken phone lay on the floor.

The student was immediately taken to the office by our coach and suspended by our principal. He was emotionally disturbed and didn't like to listen to me or any other teachers. Both of his mothers went to the school board office and met with the superintendent of school, complaining about me!

The superintendent set up a meeting with both mothers and me.

I had done nothing wrong. I had calmly asked my students to go next door. I didn't want them to see the violence my student was inflicting on me and our classroom.

I still had red marks and bruises on my arms and neck area even after several days. The mothers were still mad at me for something I had not done!

The suspension remained in place for the rest of the week. Then the boy was moved from my class!

Afterword
Golden Isles Elementary, Brunswick, Georgia

Even though my husband, Richard, was never stationed in Alaska, he was sent by his federal agency for months at a time. Of course, I never could go with him on work trips since I was teaching in Brunswick, Georgia. When he first started flying to Alaska for his agency, our twins were only twelve years old and were too young to stay by themselves.

After our son, Jason, graduated from Glynn Academy, he joined the United States Army and was ultimately stationed in Alaska. He was the only member of our immediate family to have lived in Alaska. He was there for three years!

Later in our lives, Richard and I took a three-week trip to Alaska, complete with a trip on the train to Vancouver, British Columbia, from Vancouver, Washington. Then a plane trip from Seattle, Washington, to Alaska for a seven-day cruise called the "Inside Passage of Alaska and Canada."

Dear Mrs. Smith

While in Alaska, when the locals realized that I was a special education teacher, they tried to hire me on the spot. However, that ship had sailed! I was now getting close to retirement and was happy with my life.

Years later, our son came back with his fiancée, Jessica, from Tucson, Arizona, with her parents and grandmother in tow. Jason and Jessica had asked if they could get married in our house on Christmas Eve. Of course, we said, "Yes!"

We had some close relatives who mainly lived in the Tampa and Lakeland, Florida, area. The good news was that the invited families were all able to attend. We invited a few local friends who attended the wedding. Their wedding was truly lovely. A female magistrate judge from Brunswick, Georgia, agreed to read a prayer that my brother wrote for part of the wedding ceremony. At the time, my brother Louis Wayne Novak and his wife Sandy were still missionaries in Mexico and were not able to attend.

The judge wore a lovely dark red velvet dress, and with her snow white, curly hair, she looked like Mrs. Claus! She said she wouldn't be able to stay for dinner at the time and had other plans with family out of town. However, she did stay a couple of hours and said she really enjoyed meeting everyone!

It was a lovely ceremony! Jessica brought her wedding gown from Arizona. It was a beautiful white lace floor-length gown. It was completed with a beautiful lace shawl, and she carried long-stemmed red roses. Our twin girls, Adrien and Arien, carried white long-stemmed roses and wore long red velvet gowns. We decorated the house with red and white poinsettias with red candles around the house and on the round tables covered by white tablecloths. The other women were asked to wear dresses in jewel toned colors, and the photos turned out great!

Over the years we had lots of dinners, birthday parties, and sleepover parties in that house. We also had cookouts by our pool. We updated the house and had a nice-sized screened-in room built out back by the pool. We painted the outside of the two-story house and had a new roof, and shutters put on. We had ten Christmases, many Easters, and Thanksgivings in that house and our son Jason and his wife Jessica, were married there!

Our twins left that house the day they moved to Statesboro to complete their college degrees to become special education teachers.

When the girls graduated from college, Arien left the house once again, this time forever, when she married her husband (Allen).

Soon after, we sold our home and decided to build one more house with all the latest architectural details and no pool! The kids had outgrown hanging out by the pool with Mom and Daddy. They wanted to go out to see and be seen on trips, at the beach, and have fun with their own friends, etc., not hang around with Mom and Daddy all the time.

When we moved in the day before Thanksgiving on Oak Grove Island, I thought this might be our last home. I was wrong! Two years later we were on our way to Vancouver, Washington! By this time, our second twin daughter, Adrien, was married, and her husband was finishing his masters in Savannah.

It would be a great opportunity for us both, and we knew our children would visit; however, it was difficult saying goodbye.

Both girls cried when we had to say our final goodbyes, and so did Richard and me. It was going to be a rough trip driving all the way to Washington state pulling a large U-Haul behind our new Chevrolet Tahoe. Traveling with us were our cat, Lucy, and our Boston terrier, Spanky.

The weather turned out to be awful but beautiful, with icy roads and days of heavy snow. It was so wonderful and exciting to see the mountains, evergreen trees dusted with snow, icy streams, and frozen waterfalls!

Foreword

Washington State

Washington, officially the State of Washington, is often referred to as Washington state to distinguish it from Washington, D.C.

Most Washington residents live in the Seattle metropolitan area, the center of transportation, business, and industry of Puget Sound, which is an inlet of the Pacific Ocean with many islands, deep fjords, and bays carved out by glaciers.

Washington also has huge temperate rainforests in the west as well as beautiful mountain ranges in most of the state.

Mount Rainier is an active volcano, which is Washington's highest elevation at 14,411 feet, and is the most topographically prominent mountain in the contiguous United States.

Washington is a leading lumber producer with Douglas fir, hemlock, Ponderosa pine, white pine, spruce, and cedar.

Washington is the largest producer of apples, pears, blueberries, cherries, and spearmint oil. Washington places second only to California in the production of wine.

Washingtons manufacturing industries include aircraft, missiles, shipbuilding, metal products, and machinery. Also, Washington has more than a thousand dams! Washington is one of the wealthiest and one of the most socially liberal states in the United States of America.

Rainfall in Washington varies dramatically, going from east to west. The Olympic Peninsula's western side receives as much as 160 inches of rain annually, which makes it the wettest area of the 48 contiguous states, plus a temperate rainforest. Sometimes weeks will pass without a clear day! The western Cascade Mountain Range receives some of the heaviest annual snowfall in some places. More than 200 inches!

The 9,300-year-old skeletal remains of "Kennewick Man," one of the oldest and most complete humans remains ever found in North America, were found in Washington and were discovered in the 1990s!

Before the arrival of Europeans, the region had many established tribes of Indigenous peoples, notable for their beautifully carved totem poles and their ornately carved canoes and masks.

Among their work was salmon fishing, smoking the fish, drying the salmon, and saving the dried fish for winter. Among the Makah People, whale hunting was very important. Whale blubber was used to make oil for food and fueled fires. Pemmican, a high caloric food was made into balls with dried berries, nuts, and pieces of dried whale meat.

People of the interior had a different food-based culture, which was based on hunting, food gathering, and some forms of farming, as well as much salmon from the Columbia River.

The smallpox epidemic of the 1770s was brought by the white men. The disease devastated the Native American population there.

The first recorded European landing on the Washington coast was by Spanish Captain Don Bruno de Heceta in 1775 on board the vessel, Santiago.

In 1778 British explorer Captain James Cook sighted Cape Flattery at the entrance to the Strait of Juan de Fuca. Several other explorers began exploring the recently found waterways and land.

Robert Gray, an American captain, discovered the mouth of the Columbia River. He named the river after his ship, the Columbia. The Lewis and Clark Expedition entered the state on October 10, 1805.

In 1836, a group of missionaries, including Marcus Whitman, established several missions and Whitman's own settlement, Waiilatpu, in what is now present-day Walla Walla County. This territory included both the Cayuse and the Nez Perce Indian tribes. Whitman's settlement in 1843 would help the Oregon Trail, the overland emigration route to the west, get established for thousands of emigrants in the following decades. Marcus provided medical care for the Native Americans, but when Indian patients lacking immunity to new, "European" diseases died in large numbers, while at the same time many white patients recovered, they held "medicine man" Marcus Whitman personally responsible and murdered him and twelve other white settlers. This was known as the Whitman massacre of 1847 triggered the Cayuse War between settlers and Indians.

Fort Nisqually, which was a farm and trading post of the Hudson's Bay Company and the first European settlement in the Puget Sound area, was founded in 1833. A Black pioneer, George Washington Bush, and his Caucasian wife, Isabella Bush, from Missouri and Tennessee, led four white families into the new territory and founded New Market, now called Tumwater, in 1846. They settled in Washington state to avoid Oregon's Black Exclusion Law, which forbid African Americans from coming into the territory while prohibiting slavery at the same time! After this, many more settlers traveling overland on the Oregon Trail, decided to go north to settle in the Puget Sound area near Seattle.

Finally, after arguing between the United Kingdom and the United States of America for years, a border was finally settled on by the Oregon Treaty in 1872. The border between Washington state and British Columbia holds today in 2023. Washington became the 42nd state of the United States of America on November 11, 1889.

The Cascade Range of mountains is a difficult place to live. It is hot and dry in the summer, and winter comes with a plethora of cold weather, including sleet, snow, and ice. The high mountains of the Cascade Range run north to south. From the Cascade Mountains westward, the temperatures are mild with wet winters, autumns, springs, and much drier summers. However, even in the summers, the water temperatures are cold!

The Cascade Range has several volcanoes that reach altitudes higher than the rest of the mountains. The volcanoes are Mount Baker, Glacier Peak, and Mount Rainier, which my husband, Richard, climbed with his buddies from Georgia who flew out to visit the area. Then there is Mount St. Helens and Mount Adams; all are active volcanoes. However, Mount Saint Helens is my favorite volcano.

Mount Rainier is the tallest mountain in Washington state and is considered the most dangerous volcano in the Cascade Range, due to its proximity to the Seattle metropolitan area. It is considered the most dangerous in the continental United States. It is also covered with more glacial ice than any other mountain peak in the contiguous forty-eight states!

Western Washington is home to the Olympic Mountains, far west on the Olympic Peninsula, which has wonderful dense forests of conifers and areas of temperate rainforests. These deep forests, such as the Hoh Rainforest, are among the only rainforests in the continental United States. Western Washington does consistently have more rainy days per year than most other places in the country. That's probably one of the most compelling reasons that the author who wrote the Twilight Series of highly popular vampire books, based the series in Forks, Washington. It is dark, dismal, and dreary most of the time. Sometimes parts of the movies were filmed in areas besides Forks. Forks is always mentioned in books and is their claim to fame.

They have several stores devoted to Forks memorabilia and of course T-shirts. Also, there is a big sign at each end of the small town that welcomes visitors to Forks with paintings of the main characters!

There is a Native American tribe in the La Push, Washington, community named Quileute.

Moving to Vancouver, Washington

When Richard and I flew to his interview from Brunswick, Georgia, to Seattle, Washington, we were both so excited and interested in exploring a new area of the United States. His interviews went very well, and he was hired that day!

We spoke to a couple of realtors and looked at lots of beautiful homes in the hills around the area that were in the final stages of completion.

We stayed in a nice northwest style hotel in Seattle. It was in the fall and was cold and damp! I was glad that I had brought my long black wool coat "just in case." There were beautiful displays of fall flowers, all sizes of colorful pumpkins, gourds, and Indian corn almost everywhere we went.

It was so cool that the hotel where we were staying had its windows open upstairs. The hallways had lots of windows with long white draperies being tickled by the wonderful cool breeze whispering in the long halls.

Even peering out of the windows, you could see a plethora of amazingly beautiful and colorful scenery! There were many varieties of evergreen trees and bushes. The sky was so clear that it seemed painted by a cerulean brush! There didn't seem to be a cloud in the sky and the sun was brightly shining. It was a perfect day to be in Seattle, Washington. Our hotel was situated right across the street from the University of Washington, which is known as the home of the Huskies!

I was glad that I had packed quite a few items that could be added to when needed for colder weather or put away when not. We traveled around as much as we could in our rental car and took lots of pictures. We even made the trip up to Mount Saint Helens, the sleeping volcano that had exploded twenty-five years before and changed the shape of the region. When it exploded, many homes and bridges were destroyed. Many of the beautiful evergreen trees were gone! The trees had been cut off by the extreme thousands of degrees of heat that left only stumps when the volcano blew its top and part of its side off. Now that beautiful forest was a wasteland.

Big hummocks of molten rock, sand, and clay changed the flow of the rivers in the area! Bridges were destroyed as well as homes, farmland, and animals, including a few people, who would not or could not leave the area in time.

While in Washington, we earnestly started looking for nice neighborhoods where they might have some nice homes for sale.

We finally settled on a three-story home in the hills of Felida because of the terrain; we would have the second highest elevation in the neighborhood and a great view of the community close to Vancouver.

The house was almost finished, but we were in time to change a couple of things. There would be a two-sided gas fireplace between the dining room and family room. Plus, a gas fireplace in the living room but an electric stove in the kitchen.

One more thing that I needed was a roof over the back deck; however, it rarely gets hot in that part of Washington. Some people thought I was a little crazy! I wanted the back deck covered so all my outdoor plants had protection. Lucy, our beautiful female cat, with long black fur who would travel all the way across the United States from Georgia with us, could get out of the rain and dampness when needed. I didn't want my porch furniture and grill soaked all the time.

On our trip from Georgia to Washington, the weather had started out nice but became increasing cooler day by day. We were driving our Tahoe and were pulling the largest closed in U-Haul trailer that we could find. I have always had plants, usually lots of plants. Since both twin girls were now married and settled, I gave each of them some of my plants to keep and take care of. It was still hard to fit the rest of my plants into the U-Haul trailer safely.

As we traveled, we continued to closely monitor the outside temperatures hour by hour. I love my husband so much for what he did for me! He knew I loved my plants so much because some of my most precious plants were from my Hungarian father, grandmother, and grandfather. I had to have my favorite plants! However, the only way we could keep the plants alive was by buying two small heaters that were rechargeable. We would have to check the outside temperature gauge on the Tahoe to make sure it wasn't freezing. If the temperature started dipping, we would have to find a Walmart Supercenter or some other service center to make sure one heater was always charged to maximum.

Without the heaters, we never would have made it with the plants. Even then, the plants next to the inside wall usually got a few outer frozen leaves, but all the plants survived the trip out to Washington!

While we were on the road living in hotels, we plugged the heaters in at night when we could find an outside plug on a lamp post in the hotel parking lot. Or, if not, we would stay on the bottom floor and using an extension cord connect to the trailer. When it was five degrees, even the heaters could barely get to a high enough temperature to keep the plants alive. Richard hauled some of my most precious plants into our hotel room.

Another time, we rented a very cheap room at a place and hauled all the plants in the room and put them on newspaper where they stayed for several days. We stayed in a much nicer hotel a block away. It got so cold that the temperature was down to two to three degrees for days! Most of the roads were closed because of heavy snow and ice! I wondered what the maids thought about all those plants sitting on the floor without any signs of human life in the room!

We could call for pizza and salad delivery, and the guys would always make it to our nice four-story hotel just a couple of blocks away! Richard made it to a local grocery store for a few supplies, just a block away.

Of course, living in that area, the people were used to having local highways and interstate highways gated and chained in frigid weather to stop most major accidents. Chains and snow tires were requires on occasion.

One day when we were getting ready to get back on the road, Richard threw a huge snowball playing around with me at my right-side window of the Tahoe. The funny thing was that the snowball stayed on my side window for days and nights as we traveled on and stopped at hotels for the night, gas stations, restaurants, and Walmart's. It was still cold, around three to four degrees for the high for several days! So, I even named the snowball, George, since we were traveling to Washington state, which was named after our first president.

When we finally made it to our new home, snow and ice covered the ground, grass, rocks, sidewalks, streets, and our very steep and long cement drive.

I still needed help to get up the icy eight steps to our new front door!

It was exciting to finally drive up to our new home after being on the road for weeks! It had been fun driving through high mountain passes as it snowed sideways, and the strong winds blew our U-Haul back and forth. One time, while we were driving under an overpass on slick Kansas highways covered with snow and ice, we saw a U-Haul trailer looking like it was trying to pass us.

Then we realized it was our U-Haul trailer which was about to flip over when breaking traction on the icy road. Richard was finally able to stop the Tahoe before it slid into a strong metal fence in deep snow. Another car stopped on the other side of the road while the snow was blowing hard and sideways and wanted to help the other people and asked us where the other car went. Richard explained to him that he had seen us swerving in the deep snow and ice!

Lucy, my black cat, had been lying on a comfortable quilt by herself; however, when we spun around several times and slid off the road, she jumped into Spanky's (our Boston terrier at the time) bed and sat on top of him. Neither one of them made a move or complained the rest of the day!

At last, we had all made it safely, and we were tired but happy to start our new lives in a new state with new weather and new experiences!

The movers arrived from Brunswick, Georgia, to Vancouver, Washington, as well and were waiting for us to unlock all the doors. They complained about our long, steep driveway and heavy furniture that would need to go up to the third-floor bedrooms! Their were complaints about the slick ice on the long, steep driveway!

Richard helped me get up the sidewalk to our front door and into the family room where he had placed a big, oversized chair and ottoman so I could put my feet up by the fireplace.

The weather was awful! There was drizzling and freezing rain. Later, we would have to unload the plants in the extra room in the garage. It would take a while to get to that.

Felida Elementary School, Vancouver, Washington

I was thrilled when we bought our new home. On a clear day we could see Mount St. Helens looming in front of us from forty miles away! We had a beautiful view because there was nothing in front of our home on the hill to impede the gorgeous view. Cloudy weather was a concern during the winter season. Winter brought forty-five to sixty days of low clouds and gloomy weather. Even when we were in the family room with huge two-story windows, it would still be dark and dreary!

The weather reports would even keep track of the exact numbers of days without sun! Then I knew why there were so many tanning salons in Vancouver and the surrounding area. It wasn't for a tan, but for light therapy! Some teachers told me that they had to have light therapy lamps and used them daily during the dark winter days to fight depression.

I could understand it! I went to school in the winter about two miles. It was dark and wet. Trying not to fall in the slippery melting ice and snow in the parking lot, was a challenge for sure. Then, I'd retrace my steps back home in the darkness of the afternoon with the clouds still pregnant with freezing rain or mist in the darkness.

However, when the clouds cleared, it was a glorious view! Late spring was usually gorgeous without a cloud in the bright blue sky and through the early fall days. All the flowers, grass, and trees seemed so bright with beautiful, vibrant colors, as was the sky most of the time.

Usually, it was cool even in the spring and summer. So, most people wore layers of clothing, and some teachers even wore rain boots when they took their classes to recess. When it was raining or snowing, recess was not cancelled! There was a large, covered area for the kids, complete with a concrete floor. Most kids just wore a hoodie (a hooded sweatshirt) which got wet as they played in the rain. When the students returned to my class, I had rolls of paper towels ready! The books, workbooks, and notebook paper would get damp from their wet sleeves of their hoodies!

The recess time was never canceled unless the sky was spitting hail, or we were experiencing an earthquake! If there was an earthquake, most students knew what to do—sit down on the ground, be quiet, and still—in the Vancouver area; most earthquakes were "the rolling earth" type. If you were standing when the earthquake hit, you might get sick to your stomach and even fall! If you were inside the school, go immediately to a sturdy table or desk and get under it.

Sometimes, it would rain, hail, and/or snow all in one day! Since I had just had knee surgery a few months before, I had to be careful when walking, and I still had a hard time getting upstairs. Thankfully, my school was all one level. However, our new house was three stories! The bedrooms were all on the third floor!

Felida Elementary had a great reputation, was close to home, and in a great upper-class neighborhood. I was in a brand-new pod building that had just been completed. There were six new classrooms in the pod. All classrooms had new furniture. There were five fifth grade rooms and one room for a special education class.

In the middle of the pod, there were enough long tables and chairs for the fifth-grade classes. All the fifth-grade classrooms and the special education classroom (six in all) each had new furniture. Each grade level was set up that same way. The classrooms surrounded the conference area in the middle of each pod. The classrooms had a large window and a nice door with a window in the door. Each classroom had a sturdy and heavy back door with a window that faced the back playground.

Usually, there were three or more meetings for the fifth graders in a week. The meetings would usually last about an hour. Some meetings for the fifth grade would be longer. The meetings were 4-H meetings, science fair project meetings, which were required for each fifth grader, and Boy and Girl Scout meetings. There was also a field trip meeting.

Right outside of the brand-new fifth grade pod, there were new fifth grade bathrooms, and they were always kept clean. They even had paper seat covers for the children to use if they wanted.

Each grade level had a full-sized refrigerator and microwave in the grade level pods. There were cabinets with a sink and of course, a large coffee pot for those who drank coffee throughout the day! My new principal asked me if I would check the coffee pot during the day to make sure there was always fresh coffee. Remember, we were living in Washington state, and everyone seemed to drink a lot of coffee!

However, I had to tell him that I didn't drink coffee and have never made coffee! He looked shocked! So, he needed to get another teacher or paraprofessional in the fifth-grade pod to make it correctly! He could hardly believe it!

In almost every business parking lot, there was a cute coffee shop on wheels parked close to the street with a line of cars waiting for their order to be filled by the cute baristas and It was amazing to us!

When I got the information there was going to be a black student in fifth grade and he would be in my classroom part time, I almost laughed! Mr. Jones had called me into his office and closed the door. While I was trying to figure out what indiscretion I had committed, Mr. Jones tried to break the news to me cautiously.

I assured my principal and the fifth-grade teacher whose room he would be in that it would be fine! She was nervous; she had never taught a black child. African American people aren't prevalent in the Northwestern US. The boy's name is Christian.

The fifth-grade teacher wanted me to help her with Christian. When I found out that his father was a prominent businessman from Seattle and his mother was a practicing medical doctor at one of the hospitals in Vancouver, I wasn't too worried.

I expected Christian to be like any child that was starting at a new school and was accustomed to living in a high-end neighborhood. I had high expectations, and I was not let down. Anyway, everything went well with Christian. He was an excellent student.

Christian came to my classroom before lunch. He was in my fifth grade reading and written language classes. He worked hard and was a good student but needed some help in reading and comprehension. Christian was very smart in math and science. He worked hard and had great manners.

I loved teaching at Felida! It was in the wealthiest economic area in the county. It was common for teachers to receive extravagant gifts such as free tickets for a cruise or plane tickets for Christmas, or maybe a beautiful gold bracelet or nice diamond earrings!

Every regular education classroom teacher had parent volunteers who would go to the school library/media center on Friday mornings and set up the schoolwork that had been graded, or the parents graded the work for their child's teacher and recorded the grades in the teacher's record books. Volunteers also put together the weekly lunch and breakfast menus, a letter from their child's classroom teacher and one from our principal, etc. All would be stapled together and be ready to send home each Friday afternoon. It really helped the homeroom teachers out.

Parent/teacher conference days were held every six weeks. Teachers could start at 8:00 a.m. on a Friday. When you were finished with the conferences, you were done, and you could leave for the day or schedule conferences later in the afternoon.

Usually, on Mondays after school, the faculty would have a meeting. The first order of business was to complete the form for overtime pay. Washington was a union state, so teachers, principals, and paraprofessionals were compensated for additional time.

Another thing that was different in the fall and winter in Vancouver was that the custodians would have to sprinkle road salt in the parking lots and sidewalks. So, most paraprofessionals and some teachers would wear galoshes over their shoes because of the rain, salt, and melting snow.

I was surprised when Richard and I decided to go shopping early one pretty fall Saturday morning! Neither one of us had ever seen big trucks that vacuumed the brightly colored fall leaves (about two to three feet deep in the streets) and just sucked the beautiful, vibrantly colored leaves up into a big tank on the back of the truck!

In the winter, I would go to school in the dark and come home in the dark! The days are much shorter in the winter! Even at noon, it would usually be very damp, dreary, and cold and hardly ever would we see the sunshine!

During the summer, in the evenings, the sky turned a lovely rich dark blue. Even late at night in the summer, you really don't need lights outside to walk your dogs!

On the weekends, in the fall and winter, we could always go up to Mount St. Helen, Mount Mt. Rainer, or my favorite, Mount Hood.

Usually in the winter, Mount Hood has many skiers, lots of snowboarders, and several people going up the mountain on the ski lifts and going back down by skiing.

Mount Hood has a lot of snow usually in the late fall and all through the winter months and into the spring. Sometimes the snow covers the large Timberline ski lodge from early to late fall, at least to the first and second floors. Then it was quite comical to watch only the ski boots locked in on the skis going by the third-floor windows!

Mount Hood is also famous for the outdoor scenes at the Timberline Lodge. The historic hotel was made world famous when the film "The Shining," starred Jack Nicholson. The hotel has some famous memorabilia from the movie, including the famous axe that

Nicholson was holding when he goes on a killing rampage and yells, "Here's Johnny!" The axe is embedded in a large tree stump on the first level of The Timberline Hotel. The lodge was built in the 1930s.

Russia, at its closest to the United States, is about fifty-five miles from the state of Alaska so a large Russians population existed in Vancouver. Many of the parents could not speak English and were working as handymen, lawn care workers, and restaurant workers. Many of the Russian women also worked as maids, custodians, cafeteria workers, and fish cleaners.

When I had a conference scheduled, I always made sure that the parents could speak English; if not, we would need an interpreter, and that usually was their own child. Also, my principal and/or guidance counselor would attend. Remember, I had many conferences since I was the only special needs teacher in the school except for the speech-communication teacher, Sarah.

Sarah gave me some good information about how things really worked in special education classes in Washington.

I usually had a caseload of between twenty-seven and thirty students. I was even involved with kindergarten students. We had special forms that were printed with the students' goals, and I would have my paraprofessionals with some of the neediest students in kindergarten. The students in kindergarten would usually receive forty-five minutes to an hour of special education services through my paraprofessionals daily. Once a week, the five to six paraprofessionals would test and give me results. Kindergarten was a half day. So, each kindergarten teacher would have an early class, have a lunch break, then have a new afternoon class.

Some of my paraprofessionals would work with older children in their regular education classes for an hour or two. They tested once a week and gave me the data, and I would chart it and keep it accessible in my notebook.

Some of my students were very high level but exhibited behaviors that were indicative of autism.

Also, there were the hyperactive students who could not sit still for very long periods of time, and who needed to move around a lot. So, I put a few kids on a schedule to walk to my room several times a day (even just using their large muscles in their legs helped). Then the kids had to jump on a small trampoline for five minutes, set the quiet timer, then sign their name and walk back to their regular class. It was imperative to stay on schedule, so kids weren't waiting around. The trampoline was behind a large bookcase with a quiet timer and sign-in sheet. Some of my students had a squishy rubber toy attached to their desk leg where they could mash it with their foot or squeeze it with their hand when they were having trouble listening and focusing. Also, I had bought athletic socks and filled them with aquarium gravel to put on their laps in class to calm them down, and I also had several one-legged stools that helped the kids focus.

First thing in the mornings, I had a group of older children that I worked with to help them build good self-esteem and to help them learn to get along with others. Later, I also added a kindergartener, who could not write at all. He couldn't stay between the lines and had a hard time writing any recognizable letters in his name. So, when his mom came to me one morning out of the blue and cried. She told me I was her only hope. I agreed to try and help Thomas. However, he would not count as one of my students. Since kindergarten was half day and he went to his kindergarten class in the afternoons, there would be no conflict. His mother was so relieved and hugged me. She promised to have Thomas at my classroom door at 7:30 a.m. Monday through Friday for thirty minutes a day, and she kept her promise! Then after my early morning group, his mom would pick him up and thank me profusely.

At first, I had Thomas try to follow a path between two black lines on my whiteboard which curved, zigzagged up and down, and became narrower on the whiteboard as the days progressed. Then I had Thomas pick a colored marker and try to stay between the lines on a more and more complicated design. I had one of my paraprofessionals copy a book for me so Thomas could trace the path between the lines that began to become narrower, and he began to have much more success! Thomas wanted to be able to write, and he worked hard, and it was even fun to use the colored markers and trace the curvy and zigzagging lines! I gave him a squishy rubber ball to squeeze to develop more strength in his arm and hand muscles. Then, I had him trace his name on the large white board, which got more and more narrow as the weeks went by. After a few months, Thomas graduated from my writing class! I hated to see him go, but he was ready!

One day, Mr. Jones, my principal at Felida Elementary School, came in to do an unannounced observation of my teaching skills and classroom control. At first, everything was going well, and then Bobby, a fourth grader in my class, went ballistic because I asked him to sit down during the lesson. Bobby was a cute kid but had terrible anger issues. His parents had just bought a new two-story home, and his mother told me that Bobby was kicking and using a hammer to make holes in the walls!

Of course, it was a cold, wet, and rainy day, and Bobby ran out of the back door into the cold rain. I asked my principal to stay with my class while I chased Bobby. Thank goodness, I had an oversized umbrella! I finally caught up with him, brought Bobby back into my room, and even gave him a towel to dry off. Mr. Jones seemed a little disconcerted while he sat with the rest of the students in my classroom!

Later that afternoon, Mr. Jones complimented me for being calm and collected when I was dealing with Bobby.

Another day I sent two boys, Jack and Phillip, to Mr. Jones' office. I called first to make sure Mr. Jones was in his office and had a few minutes. I had not told him about two fifth-grade students who were both nonreaders. However, he knew them well because they were often in trouble. They could not read when everyone else was reading and working. I knew Mr. Jones would be surprised when they each read a simple book to him! Remember, I had a specialist degree in reading skills and English/writing.

I knew how to teach children with special needs. After about fifteen minutes, Mr. Jones was in my room, and his eyes were huge! He couldn't believe that my fifth-grade boys were learning to read! They were both learning, and they were both proud! I let them take the books home and read to their families! One of the boys came from a large family, and every child in their family was expected to become a missionary for at least one year after they finished high school. Then, they could go back to further their education! I had given the entire family hope that Phillip would one day be able to carry on that tradition.

Christmas was close, and Jack's family gave me a beautiful wreath for my classroom door and a nice basket of goodies. Phillip's parents gave me a nice gift certificate! I had not expected anything, but I did feel appreciated.

Another day I was waiting for a student's mother to arrive for an IEP (Individual Education Plan) conference. Finally, I called the secretary at the front office, and I asked if she had heard anything from Mrs. James because we were supposed to have a conference that afternoon and she was already an hour late. Our school secretary said, "Oh, you haven't heard yet? Mrs. James committed suicide this afternoon by shooting herself with a gun! By the time her children got home, it was too late. She had shot and killed herself!"

I was shocked and could hardly believe it! She was very pretty, seemed happy, and lived in a beautiful home in a great neighborhood. She had three sweet children in elementary school, and her husband was in a high paying profession. People never know what goes on behind closed doors!

At Felida Elementary School, we would have fire drills as required. However, we also had earthquake drills where you must sit down on the ground so that you don't fall and don't get sick on your stomach!

While living in Vancouver, one night I woke up and heard banging on our bedroom door. At first, I thought someone was trying to break in the bedroom at 3:00 a.m., but then I noticed a large mirror was shaking and so was a painting. When we realized we were having an earthquake, we jumped up to see if people were running out of their homes. We didn't see anyone outside and were afraid to go from the third floor in the middle of our home because we would be trapped if the stairs started buckling! We were debating what to do, and then it stopped!

News of the earthquake was in the newspaper the next day. However, we didn't seem to have any cracks inside or outside that we could find. Our house was newly constructed and had piers drilled into the rock foundation, which stabilized it.

We decided to get a rope climbing ladder and keep it by our French doors in our third-floor bedroom. Then, if we had another earthquake, we could climb down to our second-floor balcony, then over the top, and go down to the driveway! That was the worst earthquake we ever experienced in Vancouver. Sometimes when going down or up the staircase built into the middle of the house, we would notice shaking like a wet dog was shaking! Then the earthquake would be over!

One day a teacher who used to teach at another school close to us said she had to keep reprimanding a student in her class. She said that he kept thumping the wall by a bookcase. However, he kept saying, "I'm not doing anything!" Finally, our friend believed him and realized the walls were shaking on their own, due to earthquake tremors!!

Another fun time we experienced was riding the light rail trains in the Portland area of Oregon. The Columbia River divided Vancouver, Washington, from Portland, Oregon, and on a clear day, you could view beautiful Mount Hood as you traveled over the bridge. We boarded the light rail train and rode to the "The Saturday Market" in Portland.

Over the years, we bought beautiful handmade ceramic pottery, African handmade baskets, large-framed photos of beautiful scenery in the area, homemade soaps, lotions, jewelry, paintings, lots of beautiful fresh produce, plants, clothes, and too much more to mention. When we went to the market, we would always find a food cart to order lunch from! Also, there was always exotic music and exotic women dancing in beautiful costumes. We had a great time! When friends and family came to visit, we always took them to the Saturday market for a fun day!

We also went to many wonderful concerts in Portland at the Rose Garden. They also called Portland, Oregon, the "Rose City" because of all the beautiful roses planted in the parks and along the major highways. We attended great musicals, and we saw a couple of ice hockey games.

We even shopped at a huge mall in Portland where you parked your vehicle under the mall. The mall included a huge ice rink where Tonya Harding had practiced many times over the years. The last I heard about her; she was still living in Oregon.

We also went to the history museum in Portland. One time the museum had a large exhibition from Egypt, which was traveling throughout the United States. My mother and father came to visit for a week, and they went with us. We all enjoyed our time there.

Since it was close to Christmas, we drove up to Mount Hood another day and took pictures of kids going down the hills on sleds, horses pulling sleighs with jingle bells around their halters, and kids laughing as they glided over the hills with the kids having a great time. We took some great photos having our own snowball fight!!

We enjoyed riding the train from Vancouver, Washington, to Seattle and never got tired of it! We always had a great time on the train and loved watching the scenery go zipping quickly by. We would make several quick stops at the stations and pick up more people along the way. The seats are more comfortable than plane seats, and you have more leg room and can get up and walk around some. There are a couple of bathroom cars, and the bathrooms are bigger and more comfortable than a plane. Also, there is a bistro car where we sometimes would have a late breakfast or an early light lunch with a nice glass of wine. Many times, we observed people working on their computers on the way to work or on the way back home, using their time wisely.

The train station in Seattle is at the football stadium where the Seattle Sea Hawks play their home games. Seattle is a beautiful city with plenty of famous buildings in the downtown area. The world the famous Pike's Market on the waterfront is where you can find almost anything. There are prints of the artists' paintings for sale and beautiful framed art, signed by the artists. Plus, handmade clothing, knitted items, ceramics, handmade jewelry, fresh vegetables, fresh flowers, hand carved items from wood, and from the indigenous people in the area, you could buy carved ivory and other items.

You can't forget to go to the Pike's fresh seafood market and see the people that toss the fish around. Years later, after we moved back to Glynn County, the Glynn County School Board showed all the teachers, paraprofessionals, and principals in our county the film that showed how to get along, etc. It was a short film showing the famous fish market guys how to get along for the good of all and teamwork!

When our son, Jason, and his wife, Jessica, came to visit us in Washington, they both fell in love with the area of Washington and Oregon. Washington is named after our first president, and his likeness is on all the federal road signs, etc.

Portland, Oregon, is a beautiful city. However, it can be a little wacky to live and work there! It was not out of the ordinary to see women and men of all ages with hair of many colors: dark blue, dark green, deep pink, purple, bright orange, rose-red, and so on, with their arms and sometimes their arms and legs covered in colorful tattoos. Many seemed to dress well and looked affluent. There were street people occasionally living under trees along the busy highways with a grocery cart full of mainly junk they had found or stolen from others.

Oregon has no state sales tax so, we could buy big ticket items in Oregon and then drive across the bridge back to Vancouver! Saving money is good!.

We had rich soil on the hillside where we lived, which made the lawn grass greener and thicker. The best grass seemed to be a thin bladed bright green grass, which reminded me of bright green thread. Unlike grass in the south, the grass always stays bright green, even when partially covered with snow!

Most of the year, I would complete my outfit for the day with a sweater or light jacket over a dress or blouse and pants even into May to July.

It rains a lot on the Pacific Ocean side of Washington; however, on the east side of the state, it is completely different! There always seemed to be a soothing cool breeze at night. We never needed air conditioning when we went to bed. Most nights we would still need a light blanket. We hung two windchimes that didn't disappoint on the balcony outside of our third-floor bedroom.

On the fourth of July, we were on our boat, which we had paid to have shipped by truck from a Georgia marina.

Our son, Jason, our daughter-in-law, Jessica, and Jessica's nephew, Forest, were all having a great time even though the water was so cold from ice and snow melting in the mountain streams that the water seemed almost icy!

We ate at one of our favorite little restaurants on the water. The restaurant looked like it was on a beach in Florida, instead of a river near Portland, Oregon! Boats would come up to the docks and just tie up. Then the people would happily get off their boats and pour into the restaurant. Even the summer air would usually have a slight chill in the evenings. The restaurant had heavy, vinyl curtains that could close and zip if needed. They had several small electric heaters as well. Also, the menu was great with a Florida beach flair to it, and they had nice mixed drinks and beer. The owner of the restaurant said he tried to copy what he saw and ate when he traveled. He had been to Florida for several visits.

Other people would tie their boats to the dock as well and climb off onto the restaurant's dock and go into the bar area.

One evening on the fourth of July, it seemed like it was about to freeze! In fact, we could see our breath when we climbed onto the boat! The biggest problem was that we had not even thought about it getting so cold at night in July! I did manage to find a couple of small rugs on the boat and a few towels, but it was still inadequate for five people to try to stay warm! Let's just say that we were happy when the fireworks ended!

We still had to get the boat back to the marina. Most of us went back inside the cabin to sit and huddle together while our two grown men— Richard and Jason—almost froze going back to the marina.

It was a huge event for local people to continue to blast off their fireworks that they must have paid several hundred dollars for to just see them blast off and burn!

Mt. Rainier is the tallest mountain in Washington state and is considered the most dangerous volcano in the Cascade Range, due to its proximity to the Seattle metropolitan area.

It is also covered with more glacial ice than any other mountain peak in the contiguous forty-eight states.

Western Washington is also home to the Olympic Mountains, far west on the Olympic Peninsula, which has wonderful dense forests of conifers and areas of temperate rainforest. These deep forests, such as the Hoh Rainforest, are among the only rainforests in the continental United States.

Western Washington does consistently have more rainy days per year than most other places in the country. That's probably one of the reasons that the author set the Twilight Series of highly popular vampire books and movies in Forks, Washington. It is dark, dismal, and dreary most of the time.

Many parts of the series were filmed in areas of Oregon in beautifully dreary state parks and other parts of the movies were filmed in southwest Washington. Major filming of the town of "Forks, Washington," was done on the Oregon Coast between Seaside and Cannon Beach.

An interesting fact: The city of Seattle in Washington state, was named for Chief Seattle in the very early 1850s!

Asian Americans and Pacific Islanders mostly live in the Seattle-Tacoma metropolitan area of the state. There is also a sizable Chinese community.

Tacoma, Washington, is home to thousands of Cambodian American as well.

At the time Washington state had a relatively strong economy, placing it fifth in the nation and growing by 6.5 percent per year—the fastest rate in the United States. The minimum wage is the second highest of any state as of 2021.

My favorite thing about Washington was the snow! Even if it didn't snow at our home, we could always go up to our favorite mountain, Mount Hood, in Oregon. There we would always find some snow at the higher elevations.

Getting back to classroom experiences, one unusual thing happened that I had never thought about was having to invite the divorced parents of one of my students to a meeting. Sally my student could get easily upset about small issues for most children. For example, if the lead in her pencil broke, she might scream, cry, and even throw it away! It was difficult to console her even with a new pencil!

Sally's mother, Mrs. Blake, called me when she received the letter I had mailed to her. I thought that she would just tell her former husband about the meeting with me and Sally's fourth grade education teacher. Mrs. Blake said that it was her ex-husband's turn to come to the meeting. I knew they were divorced, and since Mrs. Blake had primary custody, I expected her to just let him know about the meeting.

As I was about to end the call, Mrs. Blake asked, "Did you know that he now lives in California?" I told her, "No, thanks for letting me know." Then she gave me his number.

When I reached Mr. Blake on his phone, he told me that he would be happy to attend. So, I set the date and told him he could have the time he wanted from 9:00 to 12:00. He clarified, "from 9:00." I thought at the time it sounded a little strange; however, I set the meeting for 9:00 a.m., thinking the meeting would only be for forty-five minutes or an hour.

The meeting started on time in my principal's office with Mr. Blake, the father of Sally, my principal, Mr. Jones, and our guidance counselor, Mr. Leeds, and me.

Sally's father was a video game designer and developer for a large company in California. His daughter could certainly be quirky, and her father certainly was, as well.

As the time went by slowly, my principal and guidance counselor both said that they needed to attend other meetings and stood up and walked out.

After a while, I didn't have anything else to contribute. So, again, I tried to end the meeting; however, the father said, "You told me from 9:00 to 12:00! It is only 10:30 now!"

So, that was the problem! I should have thought about it! The father was very literal and probably had high functioning autism! People with high functioning autism usually enjoy working by themselves on intricate designs, developing computer games, playing computer games, designing new things, etc.

I finally stood up and told him I had booked another meeting for 11:00 a.m., so we would have to continue this meeting for another day and time. I felt bad about it, but I did have other things going on in the school!

Afterword
Washington State

Later, after many wonderful times that we enjoyed immensely in Oregon and in Washington, plus the wonderful people that we met along the way, we returned to Brunswick, Georgia. Richard went back to the Federal

Law Enforcement Training Center (FLETC) in Brunswick.

I decided to teach a few more years. I taught until I reached a milestone. I never thought I would attain thirty-five teaching, much less in three different states!

We continue to go back to visit our son, Jason, our wonderful daughter-in-law, Jessica, our first grandson, Skylar, and our second grandson, Avery, whenever we can go to Washington. Recently, in the spring and summer of 2023, we drove our forty-two-foot motorhome from Georgia to Washington with many stops along the way and back, for a total of 9,000 miles!

When Skylar's end of the year kindergarten school program was coming up, we flew out and stayed in a hotel for fourteen days. We went around visiting friends in the area and places that we loved. However, it was very sweet to share Skylar's milestone with our son and daughter-in-law!

My former principal, Mr. Jones, at Felidia, was now the principal at another elementary school in Vancouver, where our grandson attended. Mr. Jones saw me and Richard in the crowd and asked if we had moved back to Vancouver. I told him that we were just visiting our son and his family for a couple of weeks.

Mr. Jones said that if we ever moved back, he would hire me on the spot! Mr. Jones told us that I was the best special education teacher that he had ever worked with!

Then my sweet husband said, "Julia is certainly committed to her students who are lucky enough to be taught by her!"

The day that we were packing my room to move back to Georgia, my husband stood outside of my classroom in the hallway and watched quietly as Thomas' mom wrote a note to me on the whiteboard. At first, Richard thought she was upset with me! However, she wrote a beautiful note on the board that I would be sure to see and read when I walked back in. She praised me much for helping her son learn to write normally and was so sad to see me go! By the time I came back to my room, she was gone, and I never saw her again!

***

We still get excited about traveling back to Washington state! This time it had been two years since we had seen our two grandsons, Skylar and Avery, our son, Jason, and daughter-in-law, Jessica! It was a long trip from where we now live in Georgia in the Atlantic Coastal area of Brunswick, all the way across the country to Washington by motorhome and pulling a car. Also, since my husband is a Purple Heart Veteran from the Vietnam War, he gets a nice perk, and Richard, I, and Toby, our Boston terrier, can stay at wonderful military bases all over the country. We are also authorized to shop on base at the military commissaries.

We usually make many stops along the way and make many new friends! Toby loves to travel to and likes looking out of the windows as we drive. He has a special seat up front and is strapped in with his favorite blanket.

It is not a race, but a new adventure every time!

Julia Novak Smith

About The Author

Born and raised in central Florida near Tampa. Graduate of University of South Florida. A Masters Degree from Florida State University and a Specialist Degree from Georgia Southern University.

Married 54 years with a son and twin daughters. Retired after 35 years after teaching in Florida, Georgia and Washington State. Also, initiated a book club for teachers and former teachers on St Simons Island and Brunswick, GA.